Also by Harriet and Shirley

Glimpses of God: a winter devotional for women
Glimpses of God: a summer devotional for women

Prayer Warrior Confessions
Glimpses of Prayer, a devotional
Glimpses of the Savior, a devotional

By Harriet

Prayer, It's Not About You

By Shirley

Study Guide on Prayer

Coming Soon

Glimpses of God: an autumn devotional for women

Glimpses of God

a spring devotional for women

Harriet E. Michael
Shirley Crowder

Shirley Crowder
2 Corinthians 5:17

Published by:

E Entrusted Books, an imprint of Write Integrity Press
PO Box 702852; Dallas, TX 75370
www.WriteIntegrity.com
Published in the United States of America.

Dedication

We dedicate this devotional to
Alice Edwards,
Harriet's mom and Shirley's beloved
missionary aunt.
As an R.N., Alice nursed many back to health
in Africa and the States,
and made the MK experience wonderful
for two little girls who would someday
grow up and write books together.

Strength and dignity are her clothing,
and she laughs at the time to come.
She opens her mouth with wisdom,
and the teaching of kindness is on her tongue.
Proverbs 31:25-26

Table of Contents

Introduction

Creator God made the world in which we live. He placed the moon and stars in the sky, the rivers and ocean on the earth. He also created seasons throughout the year. Each season is defined by specific features and attributes that are common, although the degree varies depending on where one lives. In winter we think of cold weather. In spring, blooming flowers take center stage. In the summer, we enjoy warm weather, and in the autumn, beautifully colored leaves.

As Christ-followers we also experience spiritual seasons. These seasons do not come in order like seasons in nature, which come regularly without fail. Each spiritual season we experience is defined by certain features also. In spiritual winter, we think of the coldness of our relationship with God. In spring, we focus on new growth. Warmth and heat take over in summer, and in the autumn, shedding the old and preparing for difficult days ahead.

In the same way that nature's seasons serve a purpose on earth, so do the seasons in our spiritual lives. God provides, cares for, and sustains the earth, and in His faithfulness, He does the same for us. Our responsibility is to be obedient to God's commands in the Bible and to cling to the truth that God is in control.

This devotional is focused on spring—both calendar and spiritual. During our spiritual springs, we catch a glimpse of the new life we have in Jesus Christ and the renewed life that He gives us.

We pray that as you read and meditate upon the Bible passages and truths in each devotional that you will catch glimpses of God in and through everything around you. How has He provided for you? How is He protecting you? How is He teaching you?

Chapter 1

Shed Those Winter Clothes!

Day 1: After a Long Winter's Nap

by Shirley
Read Romans 13:11-14

And do this, knowing the time,
that now it is high time to awake out of sleep . . .
But put on the Lord Jesus Christ,
and make no provision for the flesh, to fulfill its lusts.
Romans 13:11a, 14 (NKJV)

Although the shortest day of the year, the Winter Solstice, is in December, the months of January and February seem to pass by with barely a noticeable difference in the length of the very short days. Somewhere about mid-to-late February we often begin to get a little more energy as we notice the days are growing a little longer. At the same time, the weather is usually getting warmer, and although the trees and bushes still look dead, we can see little buds beginning to form. It's still winter, spring hasn't really started, but we know it's just around the corner.

These things signify it is time for us and

creation to wake up from our "long winter's nap" and get ready for spring. It often takes a little while for us to get back into the swing of things and prepare for spring, particularly since it's still not really spring, but signs of spring will begin popping up, with buds on the cherry and dogwood trees, jonquils, and birds flying around and singing.

Many people will open their windows to air out their winter-stuffy homes and do their spring cleaning. Gardeners will work outside to prepare their flower beds and yards for spring flowers, shrubs, and trees to be planted, bloom, and grow.

We can also experience times of spiritual winter in our lives—those long periods of uncertainty, doubt, and even despair. When we begin coming out of that winter, it is as if we have been taking a "long winter's nap." We are still a bit drowsy and groggy, not quite awake.

Our passage today tells us to "awake from our sleep." *Vine's Expository Dictionary of New Testament Words* says *awake* is "awakening from a state of moral sloth." One of the definitions for *sloth* on the Merriam-Webster site is, "spiritual apathy and inactivity."

What do we do when we awaken from our spiritual "long winter's nap" and are still groggy, sleepy, and spiritually apathetic and inactive? We wake up. As we trust in God and are faithful to spend time with Him—praying and reading, studying, memorizing, meditating and contemplating His word—we begin to realize that the dark fog is lifting—we're waking up from our "long winter's nap," and as our hope increases, we shake off the lethargy and sluggishness caused by uncertainty, doubt, despair, spiritual apathy, and sloth.

Verse 12 tells us, "The night is far spent." So, there is a sense of urgency to wake up, daylight is coming. We need to wake up now, because we need to realize what time it is, meaning, the second coming of Christ is nearer today than it was yesterday.

So, once we're awake, we need to get ready and prepare for the future, right? There are several things we can do to prepare for Christ's return. We are told to "put aside the deeds of darkness" (verse 12). This means we are to "put off" our sin. James 4:8 says, "Come near to God and He will come near to you. Wash your hands, you sinners, and purify your hearts, you double-minded" (NIV). When the Holy Spirit convicts us of sin in our lives, we should confess that sin and ask God's forgiveness and walk in the freedom and newness of His forgiveness. Remember what God said through the prophet Isaiah, "Forget the former things; do not dwell on the past. See, I am doing a new thing!" (Isaiah 43:18-19a NIV).

We are then to "put on the armor of light" (Romans 13:12), and a couple of verses later we read, "put on the Lord Jesus Christ" (Romans 13:14). We are to clothe ourselves with righteousness. Not the righteousness of Christ we receive at salvation, but the things that will help us as we walk into the spiritual battles we face. We are to strive to be like Christ, as we "press on toward the goal for the prize of the upward call of God in Christ Jesus" (Philippians 3:14).

Once we are awake and prepared, we will be motivated to share the gospel with others and help them understand that a relationship with Jesus Christ is their only hope—here on earth and for eternity. "For by grace you have been saved through faith. And this is not of your own doing; it is the gift of God, not a result of works, so that no one may boast. For we are his workmanship, created in Christ Jesus for good works, which God prepared beforehand, that we should walk in them" (Ephesians 2:8-10).

Prayer: Heavenly Father, thank You for the strength, mercy, and grace You give us when we awaken from our long spiritual winter's nap all groggy and sluggish. Help us put off our sin, put on Christ, and in His strength share the gospel with others. In Jesus' name, Amen.

Thought for the Day: Wake up and get ready for God to do a new thing in your life.

Day 2: God Sees All

by Harriet
Read Hebrews 4:13-16

And no creature is hidden from his sight,
but all are naked and exposed to the eyes of him
to whom we must give account.
Hebrews 4:13

Spring is finally about to make her long-awaited, eagerly anticipated appearance. Personally, I'm always ready for winter to let go of her icy grip on the Kentucky world I inhabit. I grew up in Africa, after all, so I much prefer warm days to cold ones. I search for signs of spring. As I drive to and from work, my eyes naturally scan the trees, trying to discern even the slightest budding that may be starting, and my heart always feels lighter when I see anything that looks like spring might be finally coming. How I welcome trading my faux fur-lined boots for regular shoes, and my heavy coat for a light jacket. But then, in time, the reality of the upcoming season sets in . . . lighter clothing means more of me will be exposed and visible to people with whom I interact.

I'll cast off my thick outer coat that has concealed much of the true me, and I'll switch from long sleeves to short, shoes to sandals, long pants to capris, eventually making my way to lighter summer clothing and even swimsuits. Soon my winter eating habits will become apparent to all. Cold winter evenings spent in front of my television watching movies and eating buttered popcorn and all the yummy holiday treats will show up in places I wish they wouldn't.

Today's Scripture tells us that God has seen our winter eating all along, as well as anything else we may think we have been hiding from the viewing world.

Does the idea that God sees everything encourage you or concern you? Have you done selfless acts for others for which you have never received any praise? God saw your kind heart and good deeds, even if everyone else seems to have taken them for granted. Or are there some not-so-good thoughts and behaviors that you are glad no one knows about? God saw them, too. God saw it all—the bowls of buttered popcorn I consumed and every single Christmas cookie I nibbled on.

If today's key verse concerns you, there is good news in today's passage, too. Verse 15 adds, ". . . we do not have a high priest who is unable to sympathize with our weaknesses, but one who in every respect has been tempted as we are . . ." It goes on to point out that He did not sin when tempted, but nonetheless, He does understand temptation. Other passages tell us that God also knows that we humans are weak. Psalm 78:39 makes this point when it says that God remembers that we are just flesh.

We have a sympathetic, loving God to whose throne we can draw near and receive from Him grace and mercy. 1 John 1:9 tells us if we confess our sins, God will forgive them and cleanse us from all unrighteousness. Such good news.

I may yet have trouble fitting into last year's spring clothes, but it's still good news.

Prayer: Heavenly Father, You know all things. Nothing is hidden from You. You see us in all our sins and unpleasant ways, and yet You love us enough to forgive our sins and allow us to draw near to Your throne. What a gracious, loving, and patient God You are! Thank You! And thank You too, for spring! In Jesus' name, Amen.

Thought for the Day: God knows everything about us and He loves us anyway.

Day 3: Spring Forward

by Shirley
Read Ephesians 5:1-16

Look carefully then how you walk,
not as unwise but as wise,
making the best use of the time,
because the days are evil.
Ephesians 5:15-16

Have you noticed that something as simple as a change in the season often brings out the best in people? When signs of spring begin popping up everywhere and the sunshine banishes the winter blues, we seem to have a little more energy and our outlook on life is very positive. Each new season brings a new beginning of sorts in our lives as well as in nature, and often our outlook is renewed.

In the spring, most US states observe Daylight Savings Time by turning the clocks forward an hour. We call it "springing forward." Many of us resent losing an hour of sleep and sometimes it takes several days or longer for our bodies to adjust to the new time. Yet that lost hour seems redeemed as we gain an extra hour of daylight that is often accompanied by the beautiful and warming sunshine. And of course, we gain that hour back in the fall.

During the long winter months of coldness, rain, short days, and sometimes snow, we often develop a sense of lethargy brought on by our inactivity as we stay indoors and keep warm. The first signs of spring alert us to just how lethargic we have become, so we start spending more time outside and become more active.

Sometimes we realize that our spiritual lives have also become lethargic. We are not reading our Bibles regularly, we attend church but do not actually worship God while we are there, and we go through the motions of serving God without the right heart motivation.

When we realize the condition of our spiritual life, we need to spring forward into a new beginning or new phase in our walk with Christ. The type of springing forward I'm referring to here doesn't leave you with the sense of having lost anything—like the hour you lost for Daylight

Savings Time. This springing forward is a way of getting you unstuck and propelling you forward in your daily walk with Him.

Before springing forward we must first deal with hurts, disappointments, anger, fears, and other things that are holding us hostage. We must take all of these to the Lord as we admit to Him that we do not want to let go of them, and we must ask Him to help us deal with these issues in a manner that pleases and glorifies Him. While the process of dealing with them may not come quickly, our admitting them to God and asking for His help in dealing with them enables us to spring into our new beginning with confidence that He has forgiven us our sins and that He will strengthen and enable us to leave them behind. Dealing with these issues biblically helps us learn to trust God more as we see His faithfulness to help us, so we can walk in the freedom of His forgiveness, mercy, grace, and strength.

In Ephesians 5, Paul encourages the Ephesians—and us—to "walk in love" (verse 2), to "walk as children of light" (verse 8), and to "look carefully then how you walk" (verse 15). Knowing that we are God's "beloved children" (verse 1) motivates us to keep moving forward and not become stagnant.

In addition to Paul's admonition to "look carefully then how you walk," he also says that we are to be making the best use of the time, "because the days are evil." Here Paul says that we should not complain about the evil days in which we live or regret the time we wasted feeding our hurts, disappointments, anger, fears, and other things that held us back. He is telling us that God is at work in and through every part of our lives. Our responsibility is to "be imitators of God" (verse 1) as we walk through our lives. We can redeem the time we wasted feeding these things as we spring forward in the strength of the Lord.

Prayer: Gracious Father, thank You for giving us the seasons in nature. Thank You for bringing us through our spiritual seasons as stronger Christ-followers. Help us to trust You with all the things that are holding us hostage. As we see the signs of spring in creation popping up all around us, renew our passion to know You and strengthen us to move

forward into our new beginnings with confidence in You. In Jesus' name, Amen.

Thought for the Day: Our firm faith in God helps us to spring forward out of our spiritual lethargy as we are obedient to His word.

Day 4: Let It Go

by Harriet
Read 1 Corinthians 3:1-4

When I was a child, I talked like a child,
I thought like a child, I reasoned like a child.
When I became a man,
I put the ways of childhood behind me.
1 Corinthians 13:11 (NIV)

A few years ago, around this time of year, in the after-winter sale of one of my favorite stores, I found and purchased a wonderful coat. It was made of thick, down-alternative material and extended far enough to fall just below my knees. I had looked at the coat in the fall when it was selling for full retail, and knew I wouldn't pay that much for it. But at the sale, it had been knocked down to a fraction of the original price and I gleefully bought it before anyone else could.

I love this coat. It keeps me so warm in the cold winter months. There is nothing quite as wonderful as pulling this coat around me when I feel that

winter wind whipping my way. But once spring arrives with its warmer temperatures, I leave this coat hanging in my closet and choose a lighter jacket, even though it's my favorite coat. No matter how much I love it, I have to let it go and not wear it in the warmer temperatures because it simply would not be appropriate or comfortable, for that matter. I have to change my clothing choices with the seasons and move on to other things.

The phrase, *Let it go* has recently experienced a new popularity after its usage in an animated movie and a particular song from that same movie. The phrase could refer to many things, of course. It means one thing in the animated movie, but could mean so many other things when used in other contexts.

Today's key verse doesn't use the exact phrase, but *Let it go* certainly sums up the passage well. In its context, the phrase speaks of growing up and putting away childish things. What type of growth? Spiritual growth. Today's passage in 1 Corinthians identifies those spiritually childish things that we need to grow out of, namely being worldly in our thoughts and desires.

What if flowers wanted to stay in the ground as the warm spring weather prompted them to grow, instead of bursting forth out of the ground like they are supposed to? How strange would that be? Maybe about as strange as me wearing my beloved, down-alternative winter coat in the middle of the summer. Change is a part of our lives. It comes with growth, including spiritual growth.

So, pack up those winter clothes, prepare for the new season. Maybe you are not just facing a new season on the calendar; perhaps you are in the middle of a major life change. "Put away your childish ways," as Paul says. Face your new seasons with spiritual maturity, learning to walk more by faith and less by sight, and having your faith stretched as you depend more and more on God with each passing day.

Prayer: Heavenly Father, sometimes change is pleasant but other times it's difficult. Sometimes it's even painful. Help us as we experience changes in our lives. Make us grow closer to You each day. May Your Spirit open our hearts and minds to understanding Your ways as we meditate on Your word and come to You in prayer. Help us to put away our childish ways and become more mature in our walk with You and in our fellowship with other believers. In Jesus' name, Amen.

Thought for the Day: Let go and let God have His way in your life.

Day 5: Spring Cleaning

by Shirley
Read Galatians 6:6-10

We must work the works of him who sent me,
while it is day;
night is coming,
when no one can work.
John 9:4

I can still hear my mom as she pulled aside the curtains and opened all the windows in the house when spring arrived. "Whoopee!" she would say over and over between phrases she sang of the hymn, "We'll Work till Jesus Comes" by Elizabeth K. Mills. This always indicated the beginning of spring cleaning—not my favorite thing to do. As I did whatever chores I was assigned at the time, I felt like we were actually going to be cleaning till Jesus came back. When mom would sing the chorus:

We'll work till Jesus comes,

We'll work till Jesus comes,
We'll work till Jesus comes,
And we'll be gathered home.

I would often reply singing the stanza:

O land of rest, for thee I sigh,
When will that moment come?
When I shall lay my armor by
And dwell in peace at home?

I, of course, intended my stanza to ask when I could lay down my "cleaning supplies" instead of "armor." This just made Mom sing louder and with more passion, "We'll work till Jesus comes."

Mom said we needed to let the fresh air and sunshine into the house as we cleaned and got rid of all the stuff that had gathered over the long winter months while the house was closed up tightly to keep the cold air out. I always had to start with my room, which may explain why I dreaded spring cleaning.

Admittedly, it was a great feeling to walk through each room of the house after spring cleaning. Everything smelled and looked fresh and clean. Everything was put in its proper place and you could walk through any room without fear you would step on or trip over something on the floor that shouldn't be there.

Today I do not approach spring cleaning with the same excitement and passion my mom did, but I always sing *We'll Work till Jesus Comes* when I am cleaning or working on a big project.

Of course, Mom would always go on to make a spiritual application also. She would say that our hearts and minds often need a good spring cleaning—not just in the springtime. We regularly find our hearts and minds cluttered and jam-packed with sinful, useless, or unorganized things.

In the same way you approach spring cleaning your home, approach your spiritual spring cleaning. We dust, wipe, shampoo, deep clean, buff, pick up, throw away, sweep, vacuum, and mop. Let's see how we use these cleaning techniques in our spiritual lives.

How long has it been since you have dusted off your Bible and engaged in reading, studying, memorizing, meditating and contemplating upon

God's word? Sadly at times, our time in God's word is merely a quick reading to which we give little thought once we have read the passage. Psalm 1 tells us that the righteous person delights in the law of God and meditates on God's word continually.

How long have you been grieving the loss of a loved one, a relationship, a job, your health, or something else? Perhaps it is time to take your grief to the Lord and ask Him to enable you to develop an eternal perspective on these losses as He strengthens you to work through your grief and refreshes your faith and trust in Him. Psalm 30:5 tells us "Weeping may tarry for the night, but joy comes with the morning."

What hurts are you nursing and thereby growing deep roots of bitterness? Talk with God about your hurts and ask Him to help you work through them and wash (shampoo) them away. Ask Him to forgive you of any sin in your life that relates to these hurts and ask for wisdom to know how to resolve the issue with those involved, so that you can forgive each other and restore your relationship with God and with each other.

What unconfessed sin lurks in the hidden recesses of your heart and mind? It's time to ask the Lord to do a deep cleaning, as the psalmist did, "Search me, O God, and know my heart! Try me and know my thoughts! And see if there be any grievous way in me, and lead me in the way everlasting" (Psalm 139:23-24).

Once you are aware of unconfessed sin, be quick to confess, repent, and ask forgiveness for that sin. Then walk in the freedom of that forgiveness.

Do you have a vibrant prayer life, or has it become dull? Just like we clean and buff our floors, we need to buff our prayer life. It can become dull because of unconfessed sin, or sometimes our prayers are nothing more than routine words we say. Perhaps a study on prayer would help you better understand what it is and how to pray. I recommend you read and study: *Prayer: It's Not About You* by Harriet and the accompanying *Study Guide on Prayer—A Companion to Prayer: It's Not About You* that I wrote.

Mom would always remind me that we must work to continually keep things clean and in order around the house and in our spiritual lives. She would also make sure I knew that hymn meant that we are to work for God—share the gospel, help those in need, make disciple-makers, and other things God has for us to do—until we take our last breath here on earth.

Prayer: Heavenly Father, thank You for the prompting of Your Holy Spirit that leads us to times of spiritual renewal and cleaning. Thank You for Your mercy that forgives sin and enables us to walk in the freedom of Your forgiveness. In Jesus' name, Amen.

Thought for the Day: What aspects of your spiritual life need a thorough spring cleaning?

Chapter 2

Consider the Lilies

Day 1: Spotting Flowers

by Harriet
Read Jeremiah 29:11-14

*In the morning I will order my prayer to You
and eagerly watch.*
Psalm 5:3 (NASB)

When my children were young, I made up a little game that we played every year in the early springtime. I called it, "Spot Flowers," and that is exactly what it was about—spotting flowers. We searched for flowers wherever we could find them—in the ground, on trees, on shrubs, anywhere they might appear, as long as they were real flowers and not artificial, like might be spotted in a decorative wreath hanging on a door.

We played "Spot Flowers" to and from school every day in the early spring. Its rules were simple: whoever saw a flower got a point, but if one of us spotted a trash can, we could make our opponent throw away their flowers and go back to zero.

I made up the game because I have found that

my eyes naturally search for signs of spring as it approaches, especially flowers, because I'm always so eager for winter to be over. My children loved the little game and now play it with their children.

My children and I always found flowers on our rides to and from school. Soon we knew the location of every flower that might be blooming along our route. Sometimes we found trashcans too, especially on the day trash was to be picked up in any given neighborhood we might drive through. Why did we find these flowers and trash cans? Because we searched for them with all our might. We each wanted to win the game, so we put a lot of effort into our searches for the flowers and trash cans. It could get pretty competitive in the later spring when more and more flowers had bloomed . . . especially those times we happened through a neighborhood that had trash pickup that day.

In Jeremiah 29:13, God tells us that if we seek Him with all our hearts, we will find Him. I remember how eagerly I searched for flowers when I played that little game with my children and I have to ask myself—do I search for God with as much eagerness? What about those times when our search for God seems to be to no avail?

There were many mornings when my children and I would search for buds and flowers and not find them. We knew they were nonetheless on their way and would soon appear. In 2 Corinthians 5:7, we are reminded that we walk by faith and not by sight. On those days when none of us spotted flowers, we didn't despair and begin to worry that it might be a spring without flowers. No, we knew in our hearts that flowers would appear; it was just a matter of time. We walked by faith on those days and searched all the more eagerly the next day.

Learning to walk by faith usually doesn't happen when everything is going smoothly in our lives. It doesn't require faith to believe in God's love and blessings when things are going well. We see that even in today's passage. If you read it in context, you will see that the children of Israel were living in captivity when God gave this message to Jeremiah. Usually learning to walk by faith happens outside of our comfort zones.

What have you been praying about that you are watching eagerly to see God's hand move to answer your prayer, or to bring resolution to a situation that is burdening you? I have certainly had many such situations in my life. Now whenever those times come, and I find myself praying earnestly and watching eagerly for even the smallest sign that God is moving, I am reminded of those long-ago days when my children and I played our fun little flower-spotting game. Even when I don't see the answers, I know they are coming.

Prayer: Heavenly Father, we know You are there even at times when our lives are painful and You seem far away. Thank You for Your promise that if we seek You with all our hearts, You will be found by us. What a comfort that promise brings. In Jesus' name, Amen.

Thought for the Day: How eagerly are you seeking God?

Day 2: Dancing with the Flowers

by Shirley
Read Isaiah 35:1-2

The wilderness and the dry land shall be glad . . .
it shall blossom abundantly
and rejoice with joy and singing.
Isaiah 35:1a, 2

Spring is such a great time of year. As God's creation begins to awaken from its winter rest, everything around us seems to come to life and bloom. When I was around twelve or so, Mom and I were going to visit a friend. We had been seeing the signs that spring had come as the grass was once again green, the bare limbs of trees were now full of leaves, and the cherry, dogwood, and magnolia trees were blooming. The azalea and rose bushes and all sorts of flowers were full of blooms. Bees were flying from flower to flower, and everywhere you looked there were beautiful daffodils and jonquils.

I had just commented to Mom how pretty the

flowers were as they danced in the wind when we pulled up to where we would turn left to get to our friend's home. There was a house on a corner lot with a huge cherry tree and a magnificent magnolia tree, both in full bloom. Azaleas, roses, lilies, daffodils, and jonquils filled the yard. I excitedly asked Mom what kind of tree that was and the name of those bright fuchsia bushes that seemed to be on fire.

Suddenly Mom made a sharp right-hand turn, pulled close to the curb, turned off the car, opened her door and said, "Let's go dance with the flowers. We'll dance before God like King David did." She said this as if it was a commonplace thing for people to do.

I protested and said, "Mom, we don't know those people. They will think we're crazy. They may even call the police on us." This did not deter my mom from coming around to open my door, grab my hand, and pull me toward the yard. I begrudgingly gave in and skipped with her hand-in-hand into the yard.

Soon this almost fifty-year-old woman began twirling and dancing around the yard like a little girl. She danced over and smelled the roses and asked them to join her in dancing. Next, she danced over to a bunch of daffodils and asked if she could dance with them. The wind obliged and soon all the blooms on the trees, bushes, and flowers were dancing with my mom. I just stood there in disbelief at what I was seeing.

Sure enough, I heard the side door squeak as an elderly lady slowly descended the steps that led into the yard. Mom danced right up to the woman and said, "I hope you don't mind that we're dancing with your flowers." She took hold of the woman's hand and they both started dancing and laughing. As they were dancing, Mom said, "I'm Jeannie." The woman replied, "I'm Lucy."

Now Mom began singing, "For the Beauty of the Earth." Lucy stopped dancing and sang the first stanza with mom. Then Lucy said, "I don't think I've ever worshipped God so joyfully." Mom rushed over and gave her a great big hug and said, "Thanks for dancing with us."

I mumbled, "With you, Mom, not us."

To which Mom replied, "With us—the flowers and me."

Mom explained that when she saw the trees, bushes, and flowers dancing in the wind, she knew they were celebrating and thanking their Creator for their new life. They were also thanking their Creator for sending the warm and refreshing wind that allowed them to dance. She continued, saying that the flowers are showing off their new clothes that show us just a bit of the glory of God that we can see in creation. That was the first of many times we visited Mrs. Lucy, and it was not the last time we stopped in a stranger's yard to dance with the flowers. And yes, you read that correctly—we. The next time, I danced with the flowers, too.

I have thought about that day many times throughout the years. Not that Mom singing, dancing, and kicking up her heels (literally) was unusual for my mom; she did that all the time. I have thought about the flowers thanking their Creator for their new life and for sending the wind that allowed them to dance.

Today's passage is a promise for a specific people in a specific time and there are lessons we can learn from it today. After the judgment of God comes, He will restore His people and land. After the harshness of a cold winter, God brings new life to the trees, bushes, and flowers. And we know from Romans 8:19-22 that creation is waiting for the ultimate transformation that will come when Jesus Christ the Messiah returns.

The only logical response to the new birth we received from Christ, His glorious righteousness with which we are clothed and the encouragement and warmth of the Holy Spirit-inspired Word of God is to give Him praise and honor as we rejoice in these precious gifts. That worship and rejoicing compels us to serve God by loving others and sharing the good news with them.

What a blessing for me to have a mom who worshipped, rejoiced, and gave thanks to the Lord in very unconventional ways. For her, there was never an inappropriate time or place to break out into song and dance as she praised and thanked God for everything.

Prayer: Heavenly Father, thank You for the new life You have given us in Your Son, Jesus. We thank You for clothing us in Your righteousness and giving us Your Holy Spirit-inspired word to lead and encourage us. Help us learn to freely worship and praise You without hesitation, any time and any place. In Jesus' name, Amen.

Thought for the Day: Have you danced with the flowers lately?

Day 3: Consider the Lilies

by Harriet
Read Luke 12:27-32

Consider the lilies, how they grow:
they neither toil nor spin,
yet I tell you, even Solomon in all his glory
was not arrayed like one of these.
Luke 12:27

Have you ever walked through a field of lilies or a field of any flowers, for that matter? Flowers are so beautiful, but there is something especially lovely about them when they grow wild in a field or meadow. No human hand has planted or cultivated them, yet there they are, breathtaking to behold.

Growing up in Nigeria, I remember so many beautiful tropical flowers that filled the yards and landscape in the world of my childhood. There were the large red blooms of the hibiscus, the delicate purple or red bougainvillea blossoms that seemed to be everywhere, and the somewhat fragile yellow-centered white blooms of the frangipani trees.

Once while we were there, a fellow missionary passed away suddenly from acute pancreatitis. My mother asked me to pick as many frangipani flowers as I could and bring them to her, so she could put them on a cross she was preparing for the funeral. Frangipani trees are fragile, and the limbs might break easily if an adult were to try to climb them, but a nine-year-old, like I was at the time, could climb without much danger of the limbs breaking off beneath me. I gently dropped the tiny flowers to the ground and then collected them in a bucket to take to my mother. We had no florists there, but God Himself provided flowers for the final earthly farewell for this servant of His. I don't know how my mom attached the blooms to the cross, but she somehow managed. I can still remember how beautiful that white floral cross looked atop my beloved missionary aunt's casket.

Another moment from my time in Nigeria comes to mind. While driving home from the boarding school my older siblings attended, we passed an orchid growing wild on the side of the road. Mom asked my dad to pull over so we could look at it more closely. There was very little traffic on that road back then. We all climbed out of our car and walked over to get a closer look at the orchid. I couldn't understand why this was something so seemingly special, because flowers filled our world and we seldom stopped our car to view them. My father explained that it was rare to see an orchid growing wild, even in Africa.

Have you ever thought about the flowers? Jesus told us to do just that. In Luke 12, he said to consider the flowers of the fields. They do nothing. They don't punch a clock every day to try and bring home a pay check. They don't worry about paying bills, or how they will make repairs on something they own that has broken. They don't even worry about what they will eat or drink. They just grow where God planted them and let Him provide the soil, sunshine, and rain they need to grow. Oh, and they do something else—they glorify Him by blooming as He made them to do.

The lilies and other flowers of the fields are totally dependent on God for everything they need, and when He provides, they are more beautifully adorned than Solomon in all his splendor!

God wants us to depend on Him, too, instead of striving and worrying. Don't misunderstand this directive. There are other biblical instructions encouraging us to work. Ecclesiastes 9:10, "Whatever your hand finds to do, do it with all your might . . ." is one such instruction. There are also many passages in Proverbs that put work in a good light, even to the point of saying in Proverbs 21:25 that refusing to work can lead to death.

The real point in Jesus' instruction to consider the flowers is to stop worrying about things. God has it all in His hands, even those times when things may seem dire.

Prayer: Gracious Father, You have provided a beautiful and abundant world for us to live in. Help us to remember that You love us and are taking care of us. Teach us to depend more on You. In Jesus' name, Amen.

Thought for the Day: Stop worrying and watch how God provides!

Day 4: The Beautiful Dogwood

by Shirley
Read Romans 12:1-2

I beseech [urge] you therefore,
brethren, by the mercies of God,
that ye present your bodies a living sacrifice,
holy, acceptable unto God,
which is your reasonable service.
Romans 12:1 (KJV)

Signs of spring begin showing at various times throughout the States, depending on the climate of particular areas. In Alabama, I have seen signs of spring popping up as early as February when warm temperatures arrive early. By early March, everything is blooming and beautiful. All around us, we see signs of new life.

I grew up knowing that the dogwood was my maternal grandmother's favorite flower. When we were in Nigeria, Mom would show me pictures of beautiful dogwood trees. There are many legends surrounding the dogwood tree—some religious and some secular. If you aren't sure what the dogwood

God. In Romans 12:1 Paul is saying that because God provided a way that we can be made right with God, there are things we need to do in response.

Paul says that we are to consider the basis of our commitment, the mercies of God, as we think about how to respond. Here Paul is telling us to remember that we are sinful, God is holy, and there is no way for us to be reconciled to Him—except that He made a way for us to be reconciled. In 1 John we read, "See what great love the Father has lavished on us, that we should be called children of God!" (1 John 3:1a NIV)

Now what? What is our response to this mercy and love? The next part of Romans 12:1 answers this question. "Present your bodies a living sacrifice, holy, acceptable unto God." This means total commitment to God. We are to bring ourselves to God as a living sacrifice: to die to self, give ourselves to God, and live a life that honors Him. God wants the giver to hold nothing back from Him. Every day and in every place we are, God is calling us to live lives that are set apart and pleasing to Him.

That's asking a lot, isn't it? Not "In view of

God's mercies," it isn't. Let's look at the last part of our verse. Paul says our sacrifice, "is [our] reasonable service." When you realize the weight of God's mercies, the only reasonable response, the only thing that makes any sense, is for us to give God everything.

Paul continues by telling us how we are able to give all of ourselves to God. "And be not conformed to this world, but be ye transformed by the renewing of your mind, that ye may prove what is that good, and acceptable, and perfect will of God" (Romans 12:2 KJV).

We can give God everything in two ways: don't be conformed; be transformed. Don't try to conform to the ways of the world or let the world pressure you into conforming to its ways. Be transformed by the renewing of your mind through the Holy Spirit-inspired Word of God. God does the transforming. We call this sanctification, the process by which we are made more like Christ.

The next time you see a dogwood, remember the cross and all of God's mercies.

Prayer: Merciful Father, thank You for Your

mercies. Give us the power to live out our commitment to You. Transform us into people who live our lives as sacrifices to You so that You will receive glory and honor. In the name of Jesus Christ, Amen.

Thought for the Day: In view of God's mercies, what will you give Him today?

Day 5: In His Time

by Harriet
Read Ecclesiastes 3:1-8

He has made everything beautiful in its time.
He has also set eternity in the human heart;
yet no one can fathom what God has done
from beginning to end.
Ecclesiastes 3:11 (NIV)

I remember the day my moon plant finally bloomed. I saw it from my upstairs bedroom window and ran outside to snap a picture. Excitement filled my heart because I had waited so long to see this first bloom.

I had planted the moon plant in my Kentucky backyard from seeds given to me by a friend. The seeds came from his moon plant in Texas, which he started from seeds off of his mother's moon plant in Arkansas. The first summer I planted it, the little seeds germinated into plants, but they never bloomed.

When fall came my friend told me I should cut

them down at ground level and place mulch over them to protect them from the cold temperatures that winter would bring. Though they had not bloomed, they had grown to become lush plants, and cutting them back to ground level and burying them in mulch for the winter was difficult. I was cutting down plants I had worked hard to grow, destroying my carefully cultivated, difficult project with my own hands. Nonetheless, I took my friend's advice, since he knew much more about moon plants than I did.

I watched with bated breath to see if the plants would come up the next spring. Come up they did, and in year two of their growth they put forth buds. I checked the flower buds every day, so on the morning I spotted that first bloom, my heart leaped. Moon flowers are quite large, and I could easily see that first bloom from my upstairs bedroom window. It had finally blossomed.

A moon plant is a lush vine with large green leaves and huge trumpet-shaped white flowers. But there's a funny thing about the flowers—they only open at night. Because of their snow white color, they are especially lovely when illuminated by the moonlight. Thus, though they have a more formal name, they are fondly referred to as moon plants. Fortunately they remain open through most of the morning too, so their beauty can also be observed by less nocturnal creatures like me.

The success of my plant in producing its promised flower and the sheer beauty of the bloom itself brought me great joy. It took two years, but in its own sweet time, it bloomed.

Whenever I read this passage in Ecclesiastes, I think of my moon plant. There is a time for every event under heaven, and God makes everything beautiful in His time. My moon plant took two years to bloom and when it did bloom, it happened in the middle of the night. Sometimes His time is not what we might expect. Sometimes it's a year longer than we had hoped or anticipated, and sometimes the flowers bloom in the middle of the night, glorifying God in their own way, but in His time.

Prayer: Heavenly Father, Your timing is not always our timing. But Your timing is perfect. Thank You for the unique ways You remind us that

You have a time for everything. And thank You, too, for the beauty of flowers—even the ones that bloom in the night.

Thought for the Day: God makes everything beautiful in His time.

Chapter 3

New Every Morning

Day 1: New-Born Again
by Shirley
Read John 3:1-21

*Jesus replied, "Very truly I tell you,
no one can see the kingdom of God
unless they are born again."*
John 3:3 (NIV)

When I was a teenager, our youth group attended a citywide youth revival at a church in our community. Although I went all five nights, I can't tell you much about the sermons we heard or the songs we sang. However, one thing made an indelible impression upon me. There was a drama one night in which two young men enacted the scene from today's passage. When Jesus told Nicodemus that he had to be born again, the young man playing Nicodemus had the most perplexed look upon his face. You could tell he was trying to figure out what Jesus was saying. Nicodemus replied, "Man, you're crazy. I can't go back into my mom's belly and be born again."

Since Nicodemus did not fully understand how God works, he did not believe that God could work in that way. Like Nicodemus, many of us won't believe what we do not fully understand or what we can't see. Without the Holy Spirit and faith, Nicodemus could not understand how he could be born again. Jesus meant Nicodemus must come to a saving knowledge of Christ.

Later in the service, someone expounded upon the biblical principles of how to become a Christ-follower. I was already a Christ-follower and I had heard that passage taught and preached numerous times in my life, yet that night I understood it in a way that enabled me to know how to explain it others.

The Pharisees were known for keeping the law of God, not just the Ten Commandments but all the law that explained and interpreted the Ten Commandments. Yet while they followed precisely what the law said to do, their hearts, their attitudes, were not right.

When the truth of God's word pierces our hardened hearts and brings about new birth (salvation), the Holy Spirit occupies and works mysteriously within our lives to bring about changes that we will never fully understand, and our hearts come alive. He empowers us to obey God's commandments as we strive to please God through our worship and grateful service to Him.

When we are new-born again, others can see the result of God's work in our lives. When I was about five years old, I was arguing with my oldest brother Paul, whom I viewed as the smartest, funniest, most capable older brother a girl ever had. Apparently in school or from a book, he had learned the science behind wind. He was explaining it to me, and I told him I could see the wind.

He would say, "No, you're not seeing the wind."

I would argue and say, "I see the wind blowing the leaves on the trees." On and on the argument went until I ran pouting to my mom that Paul was picking on me. Mom explained that I wasn't really seeing the wind, I was seeing the result of the wind blowing, making the leaves on the trees dance or the dust spin around.

In a similar way, I can't see the Holy Spirit, but I can see and experience the work of the Holy Spirit in my life. It is that mystifying work of the Holy Spirit within our lives that we cannot fully comprehend or understand, but through faith we know it is happening because we can see the effect of that work in and through our lives. Our faith bridges the gap between our understanding and the reality of how God works. By God's mercy and grace, we are saved through faith. We do nothing to deserve or earn our salvation.

There is a wonderful African-American spiritual that I heard one of my mom's friends sing when I was about ten years old. "New-Born Again" explains what happens when a person is saved. Each stanza is a short statement of the change that God has brought into their new-born again lives.

I found free grace and dying love,
I'm new-born again.

I know my Lord has set me free,
I'm new-born again.

My Savior died for you and me,
I'm new-born again.

After these statements of testimony, the refrain reminds us that we are new-born again by God's freely-given grace that sets us free. Our being new-born again manifests itself in how we honor and obey God and how we love Him and others.

Prayer: Gracious Father, thank You for sending Your Son to pay for our sins and for sending the Holy Spirit to teach and lead us. Help us remember that we are free because we are new-born again. In Jesus' name, Amen.

Thought for the Day: Though we cannot fully understand the way God works, we are new-born again by the free (to us) grace of God that cost His Son Jesus, everything.

Day 2: New Mercies

by Harriet
Read Lamentations 3:21-25

. . . His compassions never fail.
They are new every morning . . .
Lamentations 3:22b-23a (NIV)

"Great is Thy faithfulness! Great is Thy faithfulness! Morning by morning new mercies I see." These are the words of a hymn that is probably familiar to most Christians, titled "Great is Thy Faithfulness." Many churches today tend to sing worship songs rather than hymns, but I can remember singing this hymn in the churches of my childhood. Written in 1923 by Thomas O. Chisholm, his words seem to reflect this passage in Lamentations. It is quite likely that he drew his inspiration for this line of the song from this Lamentations passage.

The song came to my mind one spring morning when I awoke to the sound of birds chirping happily outside my bedroom window. That morning, I opened the blinds and saw the sun shining brightly in the bluest of skies. Despite the fact that the calendar showed it to be early spring that day—a few years ago now—I could tell that it was going to feel more like late spring. It was going to be a lovely, warm, and sunny day. A large tree stood just outside the front of my house. I could see it from my bedroom window. On one of its branches that was just beginning to bud sat the happy bird that was singing so cheerfully.

I remember that morning because it was such a contrast to the day before when I had awakened to the sound of rain—cold but still refreshing, and a much-needed spring rain. The grass had greened up after the morning rain, as it and everything else appeared glad to have water. I too had been glad to see the rain that previous day.

So the day after the rain had fallen, when I woke to bright sunshine and a chirping bird, I felt equally happy to see the sunshine. Apparently I was not alone in that feeling. The bird that perched on the tree outside my front bedroom window seemed as happy as I was. This song popped into my mind right away: "Morning by morning new mercies I see." The last part of that refrain is so true, and it offered one of the reasons for the bird's joy and mine—all I have needed God's mighty and merciful hand had provided, and will provide.

That morning, I sat right down and recorded my thoughts in a journal I kept. That's why it stuck in my mind the way it did, even though it was in many ways just an ordinary day. And ever since then, the refrain to Chisholm's hymn and this Bible verse from Lamentations often come back to my mind when I wake to the sound of chirping birds from the tree outside my window. I find myself thinking, "Yep, me too, little bird. Me too."

What a gracious God we serve. His mercies truly are fresh every day and His faithfulness to us is indeed great.

Prayer: Heavenly Father, today we praise You for Your faithfulness. Some days You bring us rain and other days sunshine floods our lives, but through it all, You walk beside us in faithfulness. Your blessings to us are truly new every day. Help us to notice the ways You bless us, both large and small. And help us to take the time to stop and say, "Thank

You." In Jesus' name, Amen.

Thought for the Day: Look around you. What new mercy is God giving you today?

Day 3: Transformed Forever

by Shirley
Read Genesis 32:21-31

Then Jacob prayed, "O God of my father Abraham,
God of my father Isaac, LORD . . .
I am unworthy of all the kindness and faithfulness
you have shown your servant.
I had only my staff when I crossed this Jordan,
but now I have become two camps."
Genesis 32:9-10 (NIV)

Turn on the TV, look at the internet or social media, and you will see advertisements for products that claim they will "transform your life." They say if you change your (fill in the blank), your life will be transformed. These claims are about hair, skin, and makeup products, clothing, weight loss, and vitamin products, white teeth and braces, things for the inside and outside of your house, and so on.

We know these things do not bring about real transformation in our lives. But thankfully, God can. The transformation that occurs at salvation is complete, as we are forgiven for our sin and clothed in His righteousness. By His Spirit, we are continually transformed through the process of sanctification as we are made more and more into His image.

There are many Scriptures in both the Old and New Testaments that point to the transforming work of God in the lives of His people. We find in Genesis a fascinating account of God's transforming power in Jacob's life.

Jacob's very name meant *trickster or deceiver.* He was the second of twins. Esau was the first to be born, and Jacob followed immediately, holding onto Esau's ankle. He lived up to his name, especially at a time when his father Isaac thought he was near death. Jacob tricked his father into giving him a blessing and inheritance known as the birthright that Esau should have received. Esau was so angry with his brother that he vowed he would kill him. So Isaac sent Jacob away.

Isaac sent Jacob to the land of his mother's uncle, Laban, to live and find a wife. Jacob fell in love with Laban's youngest daughter, Rachel, and agreed to work for her for seven years. But the trickster, himself, was tricked. At the marriage,

Laban substituted his older daughter, Leah, and Jacob married her. Laban also offered Rachel to Jacob, but only if he promised to work another seven years.

During his time with Laban, there was a change in Jacob. Years later, when he was pressed to return to his homeland, he was fearful of meeting his brother and sent servants ahead of his large caravan of family with gifts. This time, there were no tricks. But when the servants returned from delivering the gifts, they reported that Esau was coming to meet them with four hundred men.

That's where today's Scripture reading picks up. Jacob had divided his family into two camps, thinking that if Esau came and attacked one group, the other could escape harm. Jacob was left alone that night and ended up wrestling all night with an unidentified man who was either the Lord or a messenger of the Lord. Jacob would not give up, so the man dislocated Jacob's hip. The man insisted Jacob let him go, but Jacob wouldn't let go until the man blessed him.

Through this prayer in today's passage, we can see there has been a transformation in Jacob's life.

He tells God he is unworthy of His kindness, faithfulness, and blessings. It is a pivotal point in Jacob's life, as the man with whom he wrestles asks Jacob his name. The man didn't ask because he didn't know Jacob's name; he knew it well. In giving his name—*liar, deceiver*—Jacob was humbly admitting who he really was, a sinful man.

When a person's name was changed in that culture, it signified a changed heart or relationship. Jacob was given a new name. He no longer would be known as the deceiver; now he would be called Israel, representing his new identity as a follower of God.

That's what happens when we have an encounter with God. We are transformed by His mercy and grace, and we are never the same. Since our heart motive is transformed, our thoughts, words, and actions are also different.

Numerous places in Scripture teach that we must also be continually transformed into God's image through the process of sanctification as we read, study, memorize, meditate and contemplate God's word, and obey His commands. In this biblical account of Jacob, we see God's transforming power at work to transform not only one man, Jacob, but also his family, a nation, and ultimately us. That is a significant transformation, isn't it?

Prayer: Heavenly Father, thank You for Your transforming power through which we are saved and sanctified. Give us a passion to know You better and serve You more diligently. In Jesus' name, Amen.

Thought for the Day: In what ways does God's transforming power need to work in your life?

Day 4: God's Doing a New Thing

by Harriet
Read Isaiah 43:18-21

Forget the former things; do not dwell on the past.
See, I am doing a new thing!
Isaiah 43:18-19a (NIV)

New things are so exciting. I can remember
how wonderful it was to get a new toy as a child.
Living in Africa, getting something new was not as
easy as simply riding along with my mother when
she went to a store and begging her to buy
something. Getting a new toy didn't happen very
often and required a lot of planning on the part of
my parents. Usually they bought toys while they
were on furlough in the US, and then kept them
hidden until special occasions, like Christmas or
birthdays. Once pulled out of their hiding spot,
wrapped, and placed in front of me, whether on a
gift table at a birthday party or under a Christmas
tree, they appeared glorious to me. Such treasures.

Even as a child, I understood how precious it was to receive something new because more often than not, I had to make do with the old.

New things are so special. They even smell different. If I think about it, I can immediately recall the smell of new things—a new car, a new plastic gadget or toy fresh from the package, a newly baked cookie right out of the oven. Just think of how sweet the breath of a new puppy is compared to that of an old dog.

I have a childhood missionary-kid friend who once shared how his family discovered that he was color blind. New crayons were hard to come by in Nigeria. Every fall our little one-room school received its supplies for the upcoming year from the correspondence course in America whose curriculum we followed. So, at best, we received new crayons only once a year, and sometimes even those had melted in transport. Old crayons were never discarded. We used them until they were just nubs that did not adequately do their job.

That year my friend kept going to the box of old, broken crayons for his work instead of using the new ones. His teacher, who happened to also be his mother, asked him why he was pulling from the old box instead of the new. "Because the old ones say their name," he replied. "The paper says to color the tree green and the new ones don't tell me which one is green."

"Bless his little heart," as my very southern mother would say. That year the new crayons did not have labels on them telling the color. The manufacturer must not have thought about color blind people. My friend had a reason to cling to the old, but even at that it was unfortunate, since the new ones were so much nicer.

Today's key verse tells us not to cling to the old, because God is doing a new thing in our lives. God can miraculously make all things new again. Humans can make new things, but we cannot make old things become new again. God can. He can restore what has been damaged, whether an old body or broken relationship, and He can even resurrect that which is dead. He did that very thing when Jesus died and was resurrected again in three days and He will again on the last day when we Christ-followers are resurrected to live with Him forever.

Spring is such a time of new things. Just visit a farm to see all the new life that is walking around on little wobbly legs. Do you need a new relationship with someone in your life, or even with God? Do you need a fresh start in some area of your life? Take courage; God has the power to make things new. He can do a new thing in your life, too.

Prayer: Heavenly Father, You are all-powerful. You and only You have the power to restore and renew that which is old and broken and You care deeply about Your children. Thank You. Please accept our gifts of thanksgiving and praise for who You are. Help us today with what needs to be renewed in our lives. In Jesus' name, Amen.

Thought for the Day: What needs renewing in your life?

Day 5: Arise, Shine!

by Shirley
Read Isaiah 60:1-3

Arise, shine, for your light has come,
And the glory of the LORD has risen upon you.
Isaiah 60:1

I love shiny things, don't you? Several years ago, during the summer, I was flying to a conference. It was a gorgeous spring day with blue skies and the sun was shining brightly. As I took my window seat, I took a deep breath and settled in for a restful flight. Instead of pulling out something to read or work on, I pulled out some notecards I keep in my laptop case, and before long was lost in my thoughts and note writing.

The flight attendant startled me when she leaned over the passenger seated beside me and touched my arm to let me know we were beginning our descent and that I needed to put my tray table up. We landed safely, and everyone began gathering their belongings and exiting the plane.

I headed for baggage claim to retrieve my luggage and several boxes of conference materials I had checked as baggage. A lady walked up to me and said, "I just have to get a look at the sparkly thing you're wearing on your left wrist."

As I was pulling up my sleeve, I explained it was a watch and asked how she knew it was sparkly. She told me she kept seeing sparkly reflections above my head and wondered what the sunlight was hitting. I couldn't imagine how she saw the sparkles, because my sleeve was covering the watch.

Our conversation ended when I saw my bags and boxes and I began pointing them out to the two young men who were transporting me to the hotel. I got into the back seat behind the driver. The young man in the front passenger's seat turned around to ask me a question and said, "What's causing those sparkles on the roof?"

I realized then that my jacket, made of a loose weave, was allowing the bright sunlight to reflect through onto the cubic zirconia band and produce beautifully-colored sparkles all around.

Later that evening before going to bed, my Bible reading was Isaiah 59-60. These passages were written to a particular people in a specific time in history. The Jews had not been following God and had been in captivity. In Isaiah 59:2 we see the problem when we read, "Your iniquities have made a separation between you and your God."

Then in Isaiah 59:16 we see that things were so bad God could not find even one man who would intercede for and lead His people. God waited patiently, but no one stepped forward. So He put on His armor (also read Ephesians 6:10-17) and went out to destroy His enemies.

God gives the people hope when He tells them that the "Redeemer will come . . . to those who turn from transgression" (Isaiah 59:20). The next verse gives God's covenant promises that His Spirit will stay with them and that they will have His sustaining word with them.

Now we get to today's key passage, one I learned and memorized many decades ago in church: "Arise, shine, for your light has come, and the glory of the LORD has risen upon you." Here God tells the people that after the horrible things they have experienced, the Redeemer, God's light, has come. They are to arise and shine—to reflect God's light.

Next we see that, "The glory of the LORD has risen upon you." This is a light that originates with and radiates gloriously from the Lord. God's light brings clarity, order, and understanding into our lives. The true light was manifested in the world by the coming of Jesus Christ, fully God and fully man, who would be the Savior of the world. And the Holy Spirit illuminates our hearts so we see and understand that Jesus is the Christ.

The third verse of our passage tells us that, ". . . nations shall come to your light, and kings to the brightness of your rising." Since God is speaking directly to Israel, nations would mean Gentiles. This means that when all the nations that do not follow God see His glorious light over His people, they will be attracted to God's light.

This passage gives us principles that apply to the church—not the building, but the body of Christ called the "church." The church is to be radiant with the light of God and of Christ, and to shine with the light of the gospel because the light has come and shined in and on us. In Ephesians, we read that Christ, the Light of the world, is the Head of the church (Ephesians 5:23). The church brings glory to God by revealing His glory to men, "shining forth" the life and light of Christ to everyone.

Christ-followers are to arise (get up) and go out into the world radiant with the light of God and the Light of the world so that we shine with the light of the gospel of Jesus Christ to all the world.

Like the cubic zirconia watchband sparkling when the sunlight hit it through the loosely-woven fabric, the world will be drawn to the light of God that they see shining through us as we live our lives in a way that glorifies Him.

Prayer: Heavenly Father, help us recognize Your light that shines on us. We pray with the psalmist that "Your light and Your truth" would lead us to live our lives in such a way that Your light shines through us to the watching world. Gives us a passion to arise and shine for You. In Jesus' name, Amen.

Thought for the Day: Arise. Shine.

Chapter 4

Hymns of Spring

Day 1: Fairest Lord Jesus

by Shirley
Read Hebrews 1:1-3

One thing I have asked of the LORD,
that will I seek after;
That I may dwell in the house of the LORD
all the days of my life,
To gaze upon the beauty of the LORD . . . .
Psalm 27:4

When I think of hymns of spring, "Fairest Lord Jesus" is the first one that comes to mind. We do not know who wrote the words, although we do know that Joseph Seiss provided the English translation. The words are a wonderful Christ-focused devotional as they expound on the beauty and glory of Jesus Christ and God's creation that leads us to express our praise to God.

Fairest Lord Jesus, ruler of all nature,
O thou of God and man, the Son,
Thee will I cherish. Thee will I honor:
Thou, my soul's glory, joy, and crown.

I love this recognition that Jesus is the fairest. He is more glorious, precious, and beautiful than anything else. It reminds me that Jesus is more valuable than anything.

This stanza reminds us that God created everything, "in heaven and on earth, visible and invisible . . . all things were created through Him and for Him" (Colossians 1:16). As we sing about Creator God, we call Him the "ruler of all nature" which acknowledges He is sovereign over all the world. This is an important biblical truth that shapes our view about God, by whom and for whom everything was created, and also our view of the world around us.

When we are reminded of and see God's glory, we can't help but respond to Him with our worship and express our deep love for Him. We affirm that we will cherish and honor Him and declare that God alone is our "soul's glory, joy, and crown." Basically, we are singing that we treasure Christ more than anything else.

We'll look at the second and third stanzas together:

Fair are the meadows. Fair are the
woodlands,
Robed in the blooming garb of spring.
Jesus is fairer. Jesus is purer,
Who makes the woeful heart to sing.

Fair is the sunshine. Fair is the moonlight,
And all the twinkling, starry host.
Jesus shines brighter. Jesus shines purer
Than all the angels heaven can boast.

Both of these stanzas speak of the beauty of nature. Many times I have been overwhelmed by the splendor of nature—a beautiful sunrise or sunset over the ocean, the colorful array of fall foliage, the resplendent beauty of the tulip and dogwood trees in full bloom. If you don't live in an area that has four distinct seasons, you may not be able to really grasp the joy that comes with the end of winter when we rejoice in the "blooming garb of spring" that "robes" everything. These all give just a hint of the beauty and glory of Jesus Christ, for their glory and beauty fades when compared to the beauty and glory of Jesus Christ. Although creation declares the glory of God as it shows off His beautiful creation (Psalm 19:1-2), it does not surpass the glory of Jesus Christ, through whom God is revealed.

> Beautiful Savior! Lord of the nations!
> Son of God and Son of Man!
> Glory and honor, praise, adoration,
> Now and forevermore be Thine.

In this last stanza, we recognize Christ's redeeming work of atonement and the lordship of Jesus Christ who will return one day to establish His rule over everything as Matthew 25:31 tells us, "When the Son of Man comes in his glory, and all the angels with Him, then He will sit on his glorious throne."

We recognize that while on earth, Jesus Christ was fully God and fully man, which results in our giving "glory and honor, praise, adoration" to God now and forever. Amen.

Take care that you do not receive so much delight in nature and creation that you forget to focus on and delight in Creator God. This entire hymn helps us realize that even the most precious things in this world—the things that are so beautiful—are not as beautiful and glorious as Jesus Christ. This realization compels us to treasure our relationship with God through Jesus Christ. Because of the finished work of our beautiful Savior on the cross, we can rest in His mercy, grace, love, and strength.

Prayer: Heavenly Father, thank You for the beauty, majesty, and glory of Your creation that gives us glimpses of Your own beauty, majesty, and glory that shine brighter than anything else. In Jesus' name, Amen.

Thought for the Day: As you encounter the beauty, majesty, and glory of God's creation, remember that Creator God made everything to proclaim His beauty, majesty, and glory.

Day 2: Before the Throne of God Above

by Shirley
Read Hebrews 4:14-16

*Let us then with confidence draw near
to the throne of grace,
that we may receive mercy and find grace
to help in time of need.*
Hebrews 4:16

The news is filled with stories about murder, rioting, protests, political unrest, disasters, and a myriad of other negative things that are occurring in our neighborhoods, cities, states, nation, and the world. If we immerse ourselves in all this gloomy news, it can become overwhelming. We can easily forget that God is at work in and through everything to bring glory to Himself, to bring non-Christ-followers to a saving knowledge of Him, and to sanctify Christ-followers. During these times our faith may waver, and we may even question God's grace, mercy, and love.

To guard against this, I suggest a few things we can do.

- Pray, asking the Lord to revive our hearts and the hearts of Christ-followers throughout the world and to give us a passion to be obedient servants. Also pray for God to transform the hearts of those in our communities, cities, states, nation, and the world, and of all of our leaders.
- Be diligent to glorify God in and through everything we think, say, and do, and to share the gospel with all those whom He brings into our lives.
- Receive encouragement and strengthen our faith by reading, studying, memorizing, meditating and contemplating Scripture.

I love singing theologically-sound hymns as a way of immersing myself in God's word. "Before the Throne of God Above" is a theologically rich hymn by Charitie Lees Bancroft. It has wonderful imagery about Jesus Christ as our intercessor and advocate before Father God. Some may not know that this is not a new hymn; it was written several hundred years ago.

As you read the words of this hymn, keep these three themes in mind:

1. Jesus Christ is our advocate and intercessor before God the Father. Because Jesus Christ is our great High Priest, we can draw near to God's throne of grace with confidence. Because of God's great love for us, even when we were dead in our trespasses and sins, Christ died for us (Romans 5:8). Through Jesus Christ we receive the mercy and grace we need at just the right time.

2. For those who are in Christ, there is no guilt or condemnation. In Christ, we are forgiven, and walk in newness of life. Galatians 5:1 reminds us that "For freedom Christ has set us free; stand firm therefore, and do not submit again to a yoke of slavery" to sin.

3. Jesus Christ is the complete propitiation for our sins, and He will keep us to the end.

The work of Christ on the cross is finished. Jesus accomplished everything that the Father sent Him to earth to accomplish. We are saved through the shed blood of Christ. "He is the propitiation for our sins, and not for ours only but also for the sins of the whole world" (1 John 2:2).

Before the throne of God above
I have a strong, a perfect plea,
a great High Priest, whose name is Love
who ever lives and pleads for me.
My name is graven on His hands.
My name is written on His heart.
I know that while in heav'n He stands
no tongue can bid me thence depart.

When Satan tempts me to despair
and tells me of the guilt within,
upward I look, and see Him there
who made an end of all my sin.
Because the sinless Savior died,
my sinful soul is counted free,
for God the just is satisfied
to look on Him and pardon me.

Behold Him there, the risen Lamb,
my perfect, spotless righteousness,
the great unchangeable "I AM,"
the King of glory and of grace.
One with Himself, I cannot die.
My soul is purchased by His blood.

My life is hid with Christ on high,
with Christ my Savior and my God.

All too often, we attempt to travel through our lives in our own strength, only to find that we are failing miserably and need rescuing. Because of our salvation that comes through Jesus Christ, we know that we can trust Him to be with us and lead us through any circumstance we face. Our status as His sons and daughters enables us to confidently approach His throne, not because of anything we have done, but because of who God is, and who we are in Him.

Prayer: Gracious Father, thank You that we do not have to approach Your throne of grace fearfully, but because of Your Son's finished work on the cross we can approach Your throne with confidence. In Jesus' name, Amen.

Thought for the Day: As a child of the King of kings, you can go before His throne to "receive mercy and find grace to help in time of need" (Hebrews 4:16).

Day 3: Heal Us, Emmanuel

by Shirley
Read Psalm 17:1-7

Hear me, LORD, my plea is just;
Listen to my cry. Hear my prayer—
it does not rise from deceitful lips.
Psalm 17:1 (NIV)

When we are in need of healing—spiritual or physical—we are desperate for help. We are weary of hurting and tending our wounds, dealing with overwhelming problems that weaken our faith. Remember that even when we need physical healing, there is often an accompanying need for spiritual healing. This can be caused by unconfessed sin in our lives, or it can be the result of living in a sinful world and forgetting to keep our eyes focused on Jesus (Hebrews 12:1-2). We need healing and a fresh beginning.

I love the words to William Cowper's hymn, "Heal Us, Emmanuel," *Hear Our Prayers.* The hymn really is a prayer:

Heal us, Emmanuel, hear our prayer;
we wait to feel Thy touch;
deep-wounded souls to Thee repair,
and Savior, we are such.

When we are in the midst of struggles, it often
seems as though God is not hearing our prayers.
Sometimes we have been wounded by the words or
actions of others and we allow those wounds to
fester and grow deep roots of bitterness. Here we
ask Emmanuel, God with us, to hear our prayer
asking for healing. We are also acknowledging that
healing can only come from God as we seek his
healing touch to repair our deeply wounded souls.

Everywhere Jesus went He met a multitude of
people "who came to hear Him and be healed of
their diseases." They all wanted "to touch him, for
power came out from him and healed them all"
(Luke 6:18-19).

The second stanza begins a thought that is
completed in stanza three:

Our faith is feeble, we confess
we faintly trust Thy word;

but wilt Thou pity us the less?
Be that far from Thee, Lord.

Remember him who once applied
with trembling for relief;
"Lord, I believe," with tears he cried;
"O help my unbelief."

I love these stanzas. As Christ-followers, when we recognize our weakness and propensity to distrust God's word, we look to Christ as the source of our comfort and relief. We implore God not to "pity us less" because of our unbelief.

We continue that line of thought as we remember the account in Mark 9:14-29 of the father who brought his son with the unclean spirit to the disciples, who could not heal the boy. So the father said to Jesus, "If you can do anything, have compassion on us and help us." Jesus rebukes the father and says, "All things are possible for one who believes." The father admitted that He believed and pleaded for Jesus to help his unbelief (Mark 9:22-24). There are many times in our lives we need Jesus to help our unbelief, aren't there?

The fourth stanza introduces another biblical account, completed in the following stanza:

She, too, who touched Thee in the press
and healing virtue stole,
was answered, "Daughter, go in peace.
Thy faith hath made thee whole."

Like her, with hopes and fears we come
to touch Thee if we may;
O send us not despairing home;
send none unhealed away.

Here we remember the account of the woman with the issue of blood (Mark 5:25-34). She had suffered for twelve years and spent all she had on doctors who could not help her. She had heard about Jesus, so she made her way through the throng of people, came up behind Jesus and touched His garment because she knew she would be healed. Scripture tells us that immediately she was healed.

Jesus knew that healing power had gone out of Him, so He turned around and asked who touched

His garment. That seemed like a silly question to ask, since there was such a large crowd of people around Him. But the woman came to Him so fearful that she was trembling, and told Him what had happened. Jesus said, "Daughter, your faith has made you well; go in peace, and be healed of your disease" (Mark 25:34).

When our faith is weak, and we look at the overwhelming problems we face, it is hard for us to believe that there is any hope that we can get help. The only real hope any of us have is Jesus Christ. God wants us to come to Him and honestly express our emotions and ask our questions. In our times of need we can cry out to God for help and know that He will hear us and help. That doesn't always mean that our physical issues will be healed or the situations around us will be changed. It does mean that He will be with us, giving us the mercy, grace, and strength to walk through whatever situation we are experiencing.

We long for that healing and a fresh beginning in our lives so that we can continue serving the Lord and sharing the gospel with those whom God places in our path.

Prayer: Heavenly Father, we need Your healing today. Thank You for hearing our prayers and healing us. Thank You for not giving up on us when our faith is weak. Continue helping our unbelief. In Jesus' name, Amen.

Thought for the Day: In what ways do you need God's healing touch?

Day 4: Kindly Spring Again is Here

by Shirley
Read 2 Corinthians 4:16-21

Who is a God like You, who pardons iniquity
And passes over the rebellious act
of the remnant of His possession?
Micah 7:18a (NASB)

Everyone seems to be a little cheerier, the days are getting longer, the sun is shining more—spring is here. It is a welcome relief to many of us, relief from the coldness and dreariness of winter. Spring marks the end of winter. As we see the new growth of trees, shrubs, and flowers, and hear the chirping of the newborn birds, we catch a glimpse of the new life we have in Jesus Christ, and the renewed life that He gives us. In spring I also think of Jesus' promise in Revelation 21:5, to make all things new.

We know that Creator God reveals Himself in and through creation. Paul tells us, "For since the creation of the world God's invisible qualities—his eternal power and divine nature—have been clearly seen, being understood from what has been made, so that people are without excuse" (Romans 1:20 NIV).

Thinking of spring reminds me of John Newton's hymn, "Kindly Spring Again is Here." Newton was a slave trader who wrote several hundred hymns after his life was transformed by God. This particular hymn, is unfamiliar to many people. And since we don't often use some of the words Newton uses in this hymn, I've put modern words in parentheses beside the more obscure ones.

Kindly spring again is here.
Trees and fields in bloom appear.
Hark! the birds with artless (innocent) lays
Warble (sing) their creator's praise.

Where in winter all was snow,
Now the flowers in clusters grow,
And the corn, in green array,
Promises a harvest-day.

In these verses we are celebrating the coming of spring as we sing about the signs that it is here:

blooming trees and fields, birds nestled in their
nests and singing, flowers and corn growing.
Spring signals growth. It takes the right amount of
sunlight and water for things in nature to grow. All
of these signs of spring point us to the kindness of
Creator God in bringing new life and renewal into
our lives.

> Lord, afford (give) a spring to me.
> Let me feel like what I see.
> Speak, and by Thy gracious voice,
> Make my drooping soul rejoice.

Here we ask God to bring spring into our
spiritual lives, so we will experience growth and
joy. In our spiritual lives, growth is the result of
spending time in Bible study, prayer, and
fellowship with other Christ-followers. As Christ-
followers, we find ourselves with drooping souls,
don't we? The struggles of life wear us down, and
we find it difficult to be joyful and thankful. Then
we ask to hear the gracious voice of our Lord so
that our drooping souls will rejoice.

On Thy garden, deign (stoop) to smile,
Raise the plants, enrich the soil.
Soon, Thy presence will restore
Life to what seemed dead before.

These words have double meaning. God is providing what the garden needs to grow so that the things that looked dead before will come to life. And we're asking the Lord to condescend and smile upon us to give new growth and enrich our souls. Then, His presence will renew our drooping souls that seemed dead before. When God is present, transformation occurs. This verse reminds me of King David's prayer in Psalm 51:10 (NIV), "Create in me a pure heart, O God, and renew a steadfast spirit within me."

So, while in this hymn we are celebrating that spring has come, the recognition of our own need for renewed hearts becomes evident.

Don't miss the point that the hymn begins with the realization that spring coming to end the winter is a kindness to us. In the same way, when the Lord brings spring—renewed life—to our spiritual lives, it is because of His great compassion for us. The

Lord provides for our needs as we trust in and depend upon Him for everything. He gives us the opportunity to be forgiven and to be renewed or healed. God teaches us through His Holy Spirit-inspired Bible and through the glimpses of Him in creation. God's presence brings restoration and peace into our lives.

Prayer: Heavenly Father, thank You for Your presence in our lives and for Your kindness in bringing new life and renewal into our lives. As we experience the coming of spring in nature, may we be renewed and grow through Your provision. In Jesus' name, Amen.

Thought for the Day: God's presence restores life to what seemed dead before.

Day 5: Make Me a Channel of Blessing

by Shirley
Read 2 Corinthians 5:17-21

Therefore, if anyone cleanses himself
from what is dishonorable,
he will be a vessel for honorable use,
set apart as holy, useful to the master of the house,
ready for every good work.
2 Timothy 2:21

For the last of our spring hymns, I thought we would look at one that speaks of our response to all the things we have seen about God's salvation, transformation, and renewal in our lives.

After we left Nigeria the last time and came home to the States, I would often go with Mom when she spoke about missions at various churches. In more intimate settings, there were usually question-and-answer sessions. People wanted to know about the strange foods in Nigeria, if we lived in a mud hut, what wild animals we saw, and so on.

Once, someone asked Mom what she was going to do now that she wasn't a missionary anymore. She explained that she was still a missionary, just on a different mission field. She told them the Lord had called her to share His love to people wherever she went, and she explained how she prayed that the Lord would use her to share His love wherever she was. Then she began singing the chorus of the hymn, "Make Me a Channel of Blessing" by Harper G. Smith.

Make me a channel of blessing today.
Make me a channel of blessing, I pray.
My life possessing, my services blessing,
Make me a channel of blessing today.

Mom prayed often that the Lord would enable her to be a channel through which His mercy, grace, and love would flow. The Lord answered Mom's prayer and brought many people across her path with whom she could share God's love.

Before we look at this hymn, let's think about what it means to be a channel of God's blessing. Paul David Tripp says, "When God calls you to Himself, He also calls you to be a servant, an instrument in His redeeming hands."

The first three stanzas of this hymn lead us to examine how well we are following God's commands to "bring salvation to the ends of the earth" (Acts 13:47) as channels of His blessing.

Is your life a channel of blessing?
Is the love of God flowing through you?
Are you telling the lost of the Savior?
Are you ready His service to do?

Is your life a channel of blessing?
Are you burdened for those who are lost?
Have you urged upon those who are straying
The Savior Who died on the cross?

Is your life a channel of blessing?
Is it a daily telling for Him?
Have you spoken the word of salvation
To those who are dying in sin?

When we have received and experienced the love of God and His salvation, we cannot help but share them with others. Through the questions in the hymn, we get a glimpse of what it means to be a channel of blessing:

- We are to allow God's love to flow through our lives to others as we tell them what Jesus did for us and about His gift of salvation.
- Our recognition of what Christ did for us makes us burdened for the lost and that they would be reconciled to God through Jesus Christ.
- We are to share the gospel of Jesus Christ with all those whom we come in contact, because the world is filled with those who are dying in their sin.

After examining our lives and how we can be channels of God's blessing, the last stanza reminds us of things that can block us from being channels of God's blessing.

We cannot be channels of blessing
If our lives are not free from known sin.
We will barriers be and a hindrance
To those we are trying to win.

No Christ-follower is free from committing sin and we must recognize that our sin becomes a hindrance to our ability to be channels of God's blessing to others. We must recognize our sin, repent, and ask God's forgiveness. The chorus reminds us that our purpose and prayer is that God would help us become channels of God's blessing.

Prayer: Heavenly Father, thank You for Your transforming grace in our lives. Give us a passion to be a channel of Your blessing to all those with whom we come in contact. In Jesus' name, Amen.

Thought for the Day: Is your life a channel of God's blessing?

Chapter 5
Hello, Mr. Sunshine!

Day 1: Sun of My Soul
by Shirley
Read Ephesians 1:16-21

Having the eyes of your hearts enlightened,
that you may know what is the hope
to which he has called you,
what are the riches of his glorious inheritance in the saints.
Ephesians 1:18

Today we are going to look at how God's Son Jesus is the Sun of the souls of Christ-followers. The Holy Spirit enlightens our sin-darkened hearts and enables us to have spiritual understanding (1 Corinthians 2:10). This spiritual understanding allows us to take hold of the truths in God's word as we read it and hear it taught and preached. He educates, explains, and convicts us of our need for a Savior. That work of the Holy Spirit does not end once we become Christ-followers, for He continues His work through His word that convicts us of the sin we commit.

Paul prayed that they—and we—would

recognize that we can only come to know and understand God through His word as the Holy Spirit reveals Himself to us. He goes on to pray that we would understand what all God gives us through Jesus Christ.

This understanding requires the supernatural work of God in our hearts. It will require more than just knowledge of the facts, it will take spiritual, or heart, understanding. Paul also tells us of the hope we have of God's calling—in our lives here on earth and for eternity. Paul continues in the next verse to speak of how Christ-followers serve the all-powerful God whose immeasurable or exceeding greatness works in and through them.

In many hymns, we see references to the sun or sunshine in our souls or hearts, referring to God's light—salvation—in those whom He has saved. That is the theme of the hymn by John Keble, "Sun of My Soul." Let's see what we can learn about the Sun of our soul from Keble's hymn.

Sun of my soul, Thou Savior dear,
it is not night if Thou be near.
O, may no earthborn cloud arise

to hide Thee from Thy servant's eyes.

The Son of God—Jesus Christ—is the Sun of our souls. Isaiah tells us that "The LORD will be your everlasting light" (Isaiah 60:19b). We will never walk in darkness because of the "Sun of my soul."

When we sing, "No earthborn cloud arise," it reminds us of the passage where we read about the devil blinding the minds of non-Christ-followers so they will not see "the light of the gospel of the glory of Christ" (2 Corinthians 4:4b). Perhaps Kreble is speaking of the hardening of our hearts, hearts that love "the darkness rather than the light" (John 3:19). This hardening, puts up a barrier. We become unable to see and walk in God's light.

As the hymn continues, we sing about resting safely with our Savior, asking Him to help us think of spending eternity with Him as we fall asleep. "Sleep" here may have two meanings: to go to sleep at night, or go to sleep in death.

We ask God to abide with us "from morn till eve," and we express our awareness that there is never a time in our lives here on earth that we can live without Jesus—we need Him all the time. As we continue singing, we recognize that if our need for Jesus is so great while we are living, how much greater that need when we die, for He is our hope.

As the hymn closes, we ask God to be with us when we wake up every morning and all through each day as we face whatever comes our way. And then we turn to the glorious thought of waking up in heaven where we will spend our time worshipping God.

So, how do we get the Sun in our soul? If you are not a Christ-follower, you are separated from God because of your sinfulness (Romans 6:23). There is nothing we can do to bridge that separation from God; that can only be done through the shed blood of Jesus Christ on the cross that paid the penalty for our sin and became the bridge between holy God and sinful people (1 Timothy 2:5). Once we recognize our sinful condition, we must trust Jesus Christ as our Savior and Lord and ask Him to forgive our sin and save us (Romans 10:9).

Then as we walk with Christ, His light guides, teaches, disciplines, and encourages us every day. God's word is a gift through which the Holy Spirit opens the eyes of our hearts so that we can be strengthened by and glorify God in all that we do.

Prayer: Heavenly Father, thank You for the Sun of our souls, Jesus, through whom we receive salvation, empowerment to live God-glorifying lives, and hope for our eternal life in You. Teach us to walk in the strength of Your light and power, as we trust in You. In Jesus' name, Amen.

Thought for the Day: "The unfolding of [God's] words gives light; it imparts understanding to the simple" (Psalm 119:130).

Day 2: Sunrise, Sunset

by Harriet
Read Psalm 113:1-5

*From the rising of the sun to the place where it sets,
the name of the LORD is to be praised.*
Psalm 113:3 (NIV)

This is one of my all-time favorite verses. I write it with my signature whenever I sign books for my readers at book signings. It makes the times we should be praising God so clear—all our waking moments. With the setting sun we go to sleep, so essentially the only time it is okay to not praise God is when we are not consciously awake.

But just who should praise God, why should we praise Him and for how long should we praise Him? The Bible holds the answers to these questions.

Q: Who should praise Him?

A: Everyone and everything according to

Psalm 150:6 which says, "Let everything that has breath praise the LORD" (NIV).

Q: How long do we praise Him?
A: We praise Him forever according to Daniel 2:20

Q: Why should we praise Him?
A: The Bible gives many reasons to praise God. Psalm 75:1 says we praise Him for His wondrous deeds. 1 Chronicles 16:28 says we praise Him for His glory and strength; Ephesians 1:9 reminds us to praise Him for the free gift of His son Jesus, who made our salvation possible, and Psalm 145:3 simply states that we praise Him because He is worthy of our praise.

When one of my sons was a preschooler, I used to play a cassette tape in my car with children's praise songs on it. One of them proclaimed, "Amen" and "Praise the Lord." Back then we often went to a certain Chinese restaurant after church on Sunday nights and ordered wonton soup and egg rolls. We didn't have enough money to order big meals when eating out back then, but soup and egg rolls were doable on our budget, so it became a nearly every Sunday night occurrence.

One night as we sat in our booth waiting for our food to come, this young son, only about two or three years old at the time—still young enough to misunderstand words and sometimes mispronounce them, too—suddenly stood up in the booth and started swaying his little body back and forth, waving his arms, and proclaiming very loudly over and over, "Hey man! Praise the Lord!" By the tune he was attempting to sing, I knew he had this song in his head and meant, "Amen, praise the Lord." He may have been hearing praise songs in his little head, but the restaurant only heard the cute high-pitched voice of a preschooler telling them all to praise God.

I had such a mix of feelings. I felt a little embarrassed, but it was mixed with pride at my preschooler telling the entire restaurant to praise the Lord in his loudest voice. Most of all, I was thoroughly entertained and amused. He was absolutely adorable standing there, with his pudgy little body, blond hair, blue eyes, and big dimple, telling everyone who could hear him to praise the Lord. I still chuckle when I remember it, and he is a grown man with a child of his own now.

I guess when the Bible says that everything that has breath should praise the Lord, I'm sure it included chubby little preschoolers shouting praises and dancing in restaurants, too.

Prayer: Heavenly Father, we praise You. You are worthy of our praise and we offer it to You today. Teach us to praise You in good times and bad, for changes in our circumstances do not change You. Walk beside us always, and may we not neglect to remember to praise You. In Jesus' name, Amen.

Thought for the Day: From the rising of the sun to its setting, remember to offer praises to God who made you and loves you.

Day 3: Awake with the Sun

by Shirley
Read Ephesians 5:8-14

Let me hear in the morning of your steadfast love,
for in you I trust.
Make me know the way I should go,
for to you I lift up my soul.
Psalm 143:8

I love mornings, and I usually open my eyes and am wide awake and ready to get started on my day fairly early. From time to time though, I find it difficult to wake up and get my day started because I'm very tired, or I had difficulty going to sleep the night before because things were on my mind. On these rare occasions, I lie in bed trying to figure out what I can skip doing that morning so I can stay in bed a little longer. In either situation, when I wake up, my mind immediately fills with all the things that I need to accomplish that day, and in those moments before I get out of bed, I have often already determined whether my attitude for the day will be positive or negative.

That is precisely why I need to sing the hymn by Tomas Ken, "Awake, My Soul, and With the Sun." You may not recognize the title of this hymn, but most folks would recognize the words in the eleventh stanza, which we know as the "Doxology." Most hymnals include only four of the eleven stanzas, with the "Doxology" stanza as the fourth. Let's look at these four stanzas.

> Awake, my soul, and with the sun
> thy daily stage of duty run.
> Shake off dull sloth, and joyful rise,
> to pay thy morning sacrifice.

We are to awaken and rise every day just as the sun does. When we awaken, we need to prepare for all the things that the day ahead will bring by worshipping God. David said, ". . . I will sing of your strength; I will sing aloud of your steadfast love in the morning" (Psalm 59:16). I've heard someone say the "morning sacrifice" is what we read about in Hebrews 13:15, "a sacrifice of praise to God." Then we need to renew our hearts by spending time in God's word and seeking His leadership and direction for our day.

> Lord, I my vows to Thee renew.
> Disperse my sins as morning dew.
> Guard my first springs of thought and will,
> and with Thyself my spirit fill.

In this stanza we are reconfirming our commitment to God and asking Him to forgive us of our sins. We also ask God to guard our thoughts and to fill us "with all the fullness of God" (Ephesians 3:19).

> Direct, control, suggest, this day,
> all I design or do or say
> that all my pow'rs, with all their might
> in Thy sole glory may unite.

We should desire and seek the Lord's leadership and direction in our lives, so we are told to "Commit [our] work to the LORD, and [our] plans will be established" (Proverbs 16:3). We should then surrender control of our thoughts, actions, and words to God. We do these things so that God will be glorified.

The Doxology:
Praise God, from Whom all blessings flow.
Praise Him, all creatures here below.
Praise Him above, ye heavenly host.
Praise Father, Son, and Holy Ghost.

"To our God and Father be glory forever and ever. Amen" (Philippians 4:20). A handwritten note in my Bible beside this verse says, "Doxology is praising God for who He is. When we recognize God's glory, we respond in awe and thereby give God glory for being God." Here we are praising God, the source of our blessings, and inviting all earthly creatures and all of the heavenly host to praise God the Father, Son, and Holy Ghost (Spirit).

Space does not allow me to tell you about all seven of the stanzas of this hymn, but I do want to look at two more stanzas.

Thy precious time misspent, redeem.
Each present day thy last esteem.

Improve thy talent with due care.
For the great day thyself prepare.

Here we ask God to redeem all the time we have wasted. The reference to the talent reminds us to be good stewards of what God has given us.

By influence of the Light divine
let thy own light to others shine.
Reflect all Heaven's propitious ways
in ardent love, and cheerful praise.

Here we acknowledge that as Christ-followers, we walk in God's light. In and through our lives His light shines to the world as we passionately love God and others.

Prayer: Heavenly Father, thank You for our salvation. Help us to awaken each morning and focus our hearts upon You through Your word that encourages, strengthens, and enables us to live our lives in obedience to Your commands so that we bring honor and glory to You. In Jesus' name, Amen.

Thought for the Day: "Let the words of my mouth and the meditation of my heart be acceptable in your sight, O LORD, my rock and my redeemer" (Psalm 19:14).

Day 4: Wonderful Sunlight!

by Harriet
Read Genesis 1:14-19

God made two great lights—
the greater light to govern the day
and the lesser light to govern the night.
Genesis 1:16a (NIV)

"I believe in Christianity as I believe the sun has risen; not only because I see it, but because by it, I see everything else." These words were penned by the great Christian writer, C. S. Lewis. The first time I read them, I fell in love with them. They contain so much that resonates with my heart. In this phrase Lewis doesn't just mention my precious Christian faith, he also offers keen insight into how important that faith was to him and should be to all Christ-followers—by it we see all things. It frames our thinking and our worldview. And I have to admit, I also relate to his using the sun in his quote, not just because it so clearly states what he was trying to convey but because . . . well . . . I absolutely love the sun and the light it gives. Days filled with sunshine always make me feel chipper and happy.

I was a child of Africa, after all. The sun hangs large and bright in the skies there. I spent seemingly endless days playing outside in weather that felt more like our summers in America than any of the other three seasons. I remember a particular type of sunshine there, which for lack of better words, I will call speckled sunshine. It danced through the swaying leaves of the trees under which my friends and I played and made speckled patterns on the ground around our tea parties and baby doll picnics.

Well, not all of my play was tea parties and baby dolls. I was a pretty big tomboy, actually, and I spent about as much time playing with boys as girls. My brother and his friends sometimes let me play with them. They would pretend to be fighting battles and make me the spy who hid under a banana bush keeping a lookout for the enemy. And I had a close male friend with whom I played in the mud, climbed trees, and caught lizards. But all of it was under that delicious, African, speckled sunlight.

As I have said, I love the sunlight, and because of that, I am always happy when Daylight Savings Time rolls around and it's time to set our clocks up an hour so that we will have an extra hour of daylight. I used to think everyone loved it as much as me, but I have come to discover—to my surprise—that some don't like it at all. But I always welcome the later sunsets.

I love sunshine in any form—streaking through a stained-glass window at church, peeping beneath my shades in the morning, pouring over my shoulders as I enjoy a walk or a day spent gardening in the warmer temperatures, and of course, all the speckled sunshine I so fondly remember from my childhood.

Revelation 22:5 tells us that someday in the new earth, there will not be a sun or moon. We won't need it because God Himself will illuminate the world. Until then, I thank Him for hanging the beautiful sun in the sky and welcome it every time I see it.

Prayer: Gracious Father, Your word tells us in James 1:17 that You are the Father of the heavenly lights who sends us good and perfect gifts. One of those gifts is sunshine, which we get more of as the warmer seasons unfold. For that and all Your good gifts, we praise You. In Jesus' name, Amen.

Thought for the Day: God is the Father of lights who gives us light, both physical and spiritual.

Day 5: Scatter Sunshine

by Shirley
Read Matthew 5:14-16

But for you who revere my name,
the sun of righteousness will rise
with healing in its rays.
And you will go out and frolic like well-fed calves.
Malachi 4:2 (NIV)

Several years ago, I was leading the preschool choir at the church where I was a member. In the preschool Sunday school, the children were talking about the Light of the world, so we were working on learning hymns about Jesus, the Light of the world. I decided to teach them the chorus of "Sunshine in My Soul" by E. E. Hewitt.

I always tried to explain the biblical meaning of the hymns we sang and asked them questions to gauge their understanding. After singing, we always had a craft, usually coloring or gluing something.

One evening before we worked on the chorus of "Sunshine in My Soul," I asked if anyone knew what we were supposed to do now that we knew that the sunshine in our souls is talking about Jesus in our hearts. I explained we need to tell people about Jesus. The craft our helper had planned was to glue glitter on the suns that she had drawn on construction paper. She had rays of sunlight radiating from the sun. The helper explained that the glitter looked like the shiny sunshine, and that since we had the sunshine of God in our hearts we are supposed to share it with everyone.

A few minutes into craft time one of the little girls took one of the big vials of glitter and was twirling around and shaking the glitter out all over the floor, her friends, and herself. I quickly grabbed the glitter from her and asked what she was doing.

She looked at me and said, "You mean you don't know?"

"No, I have no idea," I said. "It looks like you are just scattering glitter everywhere."

"No, I'm not," she protested. "I'm scattering sunshine."

Thankfully I immediately understood and was able to tell her that is exactly what Jesus wants us to do. As we attempted to clean up the glitter, we continued talking about scattering the sunshine.

Several days later I was on the phone with my mom and told her about what had happened at preschool choir. As soon as I told her the little girl was scattering sunshine, she started singing:

Scatter sunshine all along your way,
Cheer and bless and brighten
Every passing day;
Scatter sunshine all along your way,
Cheer and bless and brighten
Every passing day.

I had never heard this hymn, "Scatter Sunshine" by Lanta W. Smith, before. I wanted to find the hymn and teach it to the preschoolers. This proved a little difficult, since it was the days before everyone had easy access to the internet. Mom said it would be in one of the old hymnals at home. A couple of days later she called to tell me she found it. The next weekend while I was at home, I grabbed the hymnal and started playing and learning the hymn. Here are two of the stanzas:

> In a world where sorrow
> ever will be known,
> where are found the needy,
> and the sad, and lone,
> how much joy and comfort
> you can all bestow,
> if you scatter sunshine
> everywhere you go.

> When the days are gloomy,
> sing some happy song.
> Meet the world's repining
> with a courage strong.
> Go with faith undaunted
> through the ills of life.
> Scatter smiles and sunshine
> o'er its toil and strife.

We "scatter sunshine" to encourage other Christ-followers and to be witnesses to non-Christ-followers.

As the hymn keeps encouraging us to scatter sunshine, I thought of today's Scripture passage from Matthew. Jesus called us "the light of the world." We received God's light when we became Christ-followers, and, in the Great Commission, we are commanded to share (scatter) that light wherever we go because the world is in darkness. The purpose of light is to expose what is there, so hiding it under a basket makes the light of no use to us at all.

You may think it odd, but I also thought of 2 Corinthians 9:6-8, where we are told if we sow sparingly, we will reap sparingly, and if we sow bountifully, we will reap bountifully. "God is able to make all grace abound to you . . . [that] you may abound in every good work." That includes scattering sunshine.

> The point is this: whoever sows sparingly will also reap sparingly, and whoever sows bountifully will also reap bountifully. Each one must give as he has decided in his heart, not reluctantly or under compulsion, for God loves a cheerful giver. And God is able to

make all grace abound to you, so that having all sufficiency in all things at all times, you may abound in every good work (2 Corinthians 9:6-8).

I guess I made the connection between sowing (scattering) sparingly and sowing bountifully. You really can't go around scattering sunshine if you aren't joyful and thankful.

Galatians 6:9-10 also came to mind. Sometimes as Christ-followers we get weary of scattering sunshine and seeing little to no results in the people on whom we scatter the sunshine. These verses remind us to "not grow weary of doing good, for in due season we will reap." Remember, our job is to scatter sunshine; the job of the Holy Spirit is to transform hearts.

Prayer: Gracious Father, we thank You for giving us Your light. Help us scatter sunshine everywhere we go so that You will be glorified, that non-Christ-followers will see Your light shining through us, and that Christ-followers would be encouraged. In Jesus' name, Amen.

Thought for the Day: Remember to scatter sunshine all along your way.

Chapter 6:

Springtime Fun

Day 1: Changed in a Moment
by Harriet
Read 1 Corinthians 15:50-58

Behold, I tell you a mystery,
we will not all sleep, but we will all be changed . . .
1 Corinthians 15:51 (NASB)

"Mom, I caught some tadpoles. Can I keep them? Please, Mom, please?"

My then twelve-year-old son exclaimed these words as he ran through the front door of our house holding a jar of murky creek water in his hands. The grin on his face stretched from ear to ear and his eyes danced with excitement. I could immediately see the reason for his enthusiasm. Through the glass jar, despite the murky water, I could see wiggly little tadpoles swimming all around.

My son had been playing in a nearby creek on that warm spring day and had managed to catch five small grayish-colored tadpoles. I was not as enthused as he about the idea of keeping the tadpoles, because I feared they would die in our care. But my son was adamant and quickly began researching how to keep tadpoles—what to feed them, what type of environment to place them in, all of which he just as quickly shared with me. Finally, because he seemed so sure he could care for the critters, I reluctantly agreed to let him keep his newfound pets.

What fun we had that spring. We changed the tadpole water regularly, taking care to dechlorinate the new water, and we fed them lettuce that had been boiled for ten minutes and then frozen, as the information on the internet had suggested. It worked. Over the course of a few weeks, our tadpoles grew back legs first, and then front ones. At long last, they lost their tails. Their color altered, too, as they changed into small, bright green tree toads. My son had put a large rock in the small container where he kept them, so they would have something to climb on once they formed legs. At the point when they fully became toads, he trekked back to the nearby creek and placed them at the base of a tree near it.

The Scriptures tell us that if we are believers, we too will someday be changed. Like the tadpoles, we will also become entirely new creatures from what we are now. However, we will not change slowly, like my son's tadpoles did. No, our change will be quick, in a moment, in the twinkling of an eye. We will change from perishable to imperishable, from mortal to immortal.

The little green tree toads that we turned loose at the base of a tree did not look or function anything like the tadpoles they had been before their change. Everything about them was different. So different, in fact, that my son and I could not begin to tell you which toad had come from which tadpole.

None of us really know what our new, imperishable bodies will look like, but the Bible tells us some things about it. They will differ from our physical bodies in some significant ways—we will no longer hunger or thirst or have physical pain or death, according to Revelation 7:14-16 and Revelation 21:4. Yet at the same time, 1 Thessalonians 2:19-20 indicates that Paul expected that in heaven he would recognize the Thessalonian Christians to whom he had ministered on earth. Paul also spoke of heaven when he wrote in 1

Corinthians 13:12, ". . . then I shall know fully, even as I have been fully known." So apparently, some things about us will remain familiar enough to be recognizable to others who have known us.

I do not know exactly what our change will entail, but that we will change in a moment from perishable to imperishable is certain. What exciting news. I wonder if God will have as much fun watching us change as my son and I had watching his tadpoles change?

Prayer: Heavenly Father, we are excited about spending eternity with You. Thank You for that glorious day when we will change from perishable to imperishable, from mortal to immortal. Make us live in a way that reflects our readiness for that day to come. In Jesus' name, Amen.

Thought for the Day: We have an eternal destination where old things will pass away, all things will become new, and we will be changed into the likeness of Jesus.

Day 2: Showers of Blessing

by Shirley
Read 2 Corinthians 4:16-18

Will you not revive us again,
that your people may rejoice in you?
Psalm 85:6

In Nigeria there are two seasons: the rainy season and the dry season. During the rainy season it rained almost all the time, day and night. During the dry season it never rained. As the dry season lingered, I would hear Mom talking to people about how much we needed rain. I remember watching and listening as the first rain approached our home on the hospital compound. As it approached, it looked as though the dust was ushering in the rain as it swirled around in front of the rain. You could smell the rain coming. What sweet and fun memories I have of us—children and adults—dancing and singing and playing in that first wonderful rainfall of the season.

Many years ago, we had a drought in Alabama

and we were restricted in the ways we could use water as well as the hours during which we could use it. It was hot—the lawns, flowers, and vegetable gardens were dying, the ground was parched, and we were miserable. Mom kept reminding everyone who came across her path to pray for rain.

One Sunday afternoon as Mom and I were doing the lunch dishes, we thought we heard thunder, so the whole family went outside to listen and to look for signs of rain. Nothing. The sun was shining brightly. Disappointed, we went back inside where it was cool.

About two weeks later while traveling home from visiting family in Montgomery, we stopped for gasoline. While Dad filled the car, Mom, Tim, and I went in to get us all something to drink. As we walked outside, Dad commented that clouds were gathering. Before he got those words out of his mouth, it started raining. Mom handed me her purse and drink and started dancing in the rain as she sang the chorus of the hymn, "Showers of Blessing" by D. W. Whittle:

Showers of blessing,
Showers of blessing we need;
Mercy drops 'round us are falling,
But for the showers we plead.

You can just imagine the looks she got from the other people who were there. Mom didn't care because she was grateful for the rain. After singing the chorus a couple of times she had to get into her suitcase to find dry clothes to wear. Let's look at the stanzas of "Showers of Blessing":

There shall be showers of blessing;
this is the promise of love.
There shall be seasons refreshing,
sent from the Savior above.

There shall be showers of blessing—
precious reviving again.
Over the hills and the valleys,
sound of abundance of rain.

There shall be showers of blessing.
Send them upon us, O Lord.

Grant to us now a refreshing.
Come and now honor Thy word.

There shall be showers of blessing;
oh, that today they might fall
now as to God we're confessing,
now as on Jesus we call.

What reminders of biblical truth do we find in this hymn? We are reminded that because of God's glory and excellence, He has given us "precious and very great promises" that help us become more like Him as we fight our sinful desires (2 Peter 1:4). We must know God well in order to trust His promises. Ephesians 1:3 tells us that God blesses us with spiritual blessings. These blessings will be seasons of refreshing, as we find in 2 Corinthians 4:16, "So we do not lose heart . . . our inner self is being renewed day by day." These blessings come from God, as James 1:17 tells us.

We should pray as Habakkuk prayed, that God would revive His work (Habakkuk 3:2). Also, we should pray that God would revive our own hearts. God will rain revival upon us when we pray.

In Acts, Peter encouraged the people to "Repent therefore, and turn back, that your sins may be blotted out, that times of refreshing may come from the presence of the Lord" (Acts 3:19-20a). We experience times of refreshing when we spend time with God praying and reading, studying, memorizing, meditating and contemplating on Scripture.

Prayer: Heavenly Father, thank You for the promised blessings that You shower on us. May we be refreshed and renewed so that we may better serve You. In Jesus' name, Amen.

Thought for the Day: Are you pleading with God for showers of His blessings?

Day 3: Pigtails and Picnics

by Harriet
Read Mark 10:13-16

When I was a child, I talked like a child,
I thought like a child,
I reasoned like a child. When I became a man,
I put the ways of childhood behind me.
1 Corinthians 13:11 (NIV)

As a little girl I loved to wear my hair tied up in pigtails on the sides of my head. My older sister had beautiful, long, straight hair that she could pull to the back of her head and tie into a ponytail. Her ponytail swooshed back and forth as she walked, much like the long tail of a horse or pony. My hair was a different story. Thick and full of body, it seemed to have a mind of its own and was often difficult to control. The few times I attempted to grow it long, it did not hang straight like my sister's. It rippled in the back instead, which was not the style back then. Eventually I cut it short and have worn it short ever since. But as a child, I remember parting my hair in the middle and pulling it into ties on either side of my head. I would then put wide ribbons around these pigtails and tie them into brightly colored bows.

These are things I never do anymore. I never wear pigtails or big hair bows as an adult, but oh, how I loved them when I was a child.

I used to love to go on picnics too, especially in the spring. Somewhere along the way I read a book in which the characters went on picnics, and it planted the thought in my mind. I had a little basket in which I packed sandwiches and other lunch foods to take on my picnics on warm clear spring days, after a winter of being shut inside. I remember spreading a towel on the ground of my backyard and eating my lunch out there, often. I usually brought a friend along in the form of a doll or stuffed animal to keep me company.

Although I could still go on picnics today, as an adult, I seldom do. And I certainly never bring dolls or stuffed animals with me. These are things I have "put behind me," as our key verse says. Putting childhood ways behind us is good, for the most part. We are even instructed to do so in this passage. But there are some childhood ways in which we could and should still enjoy. The freshness of a new day, the joy of new life that spring brings, a childlike wonder for the world around us and the blessings God brings are just some of the childhood things we should hold on to.

The humility of a child is another aspect of childhood we are instructed to retain. Jesus made this point in Matthew 18:3-4 when the disciples asked Him who would be the greatest in the kingdom of heaven. He had a child standing next to Him, and He answered, "Truly I tell you, unless you change and become like little children, you will never enter the kingdom of heaven. Therefore, whoever takes the lowly position of this child is the greatest in the kingdom of heaven" (NIV).

Springtime always has me feeling like a child again. Because I was reared in a tropical country, I am more keenly aware of how my adult years differ from my childhood years during the colder months. When the world begins to warm up, my heart thrills to the higher temperatures and childhood memories flow. Although I had those little outdoor picnics in Nigeria on occasion, I especially remember them from my first few years back in the USA. Those were difficult years as I adjusted to leaving all I had ever known and loved back in Africa and tried to learn to love my new home in America . . . or at least to like it. Having a picnic in my backyard by myself—or with my little sister or a toy friend—brought some joy to my otherwise lonely world.

Pigtails and picnics by myself in my own backyard are childhood ways I have put behind me. The fond memories do warm my heart, but it is appropriate to have put them behind me. The faith and humility of a child, not so much. I hope you and I will always hold on to that.

Prayer: Heavenly Father, You give us good things to enjoy like springtime, warmer weather, and sweet childhood memories. May we learn to put our childish ways behind us as we mature as believers, but at the same time, help us to hold tight to the faith and humility of children as we learn to trust You completely and accept Your will rather than forcing our own. In Jesus' name, Amen.

Thought for the Day: Do you find it difficult to mature in your walk with Christ while also holding on to childlike faith and humility?

Day 4: Sowing Musical Seeds

by Shirley
Read 1 Corinthians 3:3-9

I planted, Apollos watered, but God gave the growth.
1 Corinthians 3:6

If you're like me, when spring arrives you seem to have a little more energy and feel better. It is as if the sunshine that is waking up everything in creation is also waking me up. And what a great time to think about the sunshine that God brings into our souls.

In spring I find myself humming and singing many of the hymns that my parents loved to sing. Sometimes I'm not even aware I'm humming or singing until someone asks me what I'm humming or tells me they love what I'm humming or singing. So many hymns—old and new—are rich with deep theological truths about God and assist us in praising Him.

Music is one of the ways that I worship God as

I express my praise, gratitude, and thanksgiving to Him. It is also a source of comfort and strength for me. And music is a manifestation of the joy of the Lord in my soul.

As I was growing up, I didn't realize the importance and meaning of the hymns I heard Mom and Dad sing and play. As they sang, Mom and Dad were strengthening their faith, planting new seeds of faith in their souls, being strengthened and encouraged to keep on going, and worshipping God. I learned so much biblical truth through these hymns.

I was well into my thirties before I realized that as they taught me all those hymns, they were teaching me who God is, what He requires of me, and how I am to worship and serve Him. These hymns taught me that God is holy, He is faithful, He is love, He is my Savior and Lord, and so many other things. I learned that when things get tough and I am stressed out, that I can take my concerns to God. Room won't allow me to keep listing all the things that I learned from these hymns. I believe my parents were planting God's word in my soul and seeds of faith that, by God's mercy and grace, have grown and borne fruit in my life.

In today's Scripture passage, we know that Paul planted seeds of God's word, Apollos watered those seeds as he continued the teaching, and God caused the seeds of God's word to bloom and grow into strong faith.

There is a little-known hymn written by William A. Ogden, "Sowing the Precious Seed," that clearly and beautifully depicts what I am writing about.

> Sowing the precious seed
> in the early dawn of morning.
> Sowing the precious seed
> in the noonday fair.
> Sowing the precious seed
> for the youthful heart's adorning.
> Sowing the precious seed
> with a tender care.

Through all of those hymns, mom and dad planted (sowed) seeds of God's word and faith in my heart from the time I was a tiny baby. They took care of the seeds they planted.

Sowing the precious seed,
sowing the precious seed.
Scattering far and wide
with patient, loving hand.
Breaking the bread of life,
telling o'er the gospel story.
Sowing the precious seed
in the dear homeland.

My parents understood that they had to scatter those seeds "far and wide, with patient, loving hands" as they taught me God's word and told me the old, old, story of Jesus. They planted those seeds of God's word and faith with a sense of urgency that I would come to know and understand my need for the Savior. They never fretted over whether I was listening or getting it. They knew their job was to teach me God's word, then they prayed and trusted God to bring that word to life in my life.

Sowing the precious seed
with an earnest, true endeavor.
Sowing the precious seed

of the golden grain.
Sowing the precious seed
and the hand withholding never.
Praying that God will send
it the sun and rain.

My parents knew they were planting the very Word of God in my soul, so they were consistent, generous, and gracious as they planted those seeds, all the time praying that God would send His light and His word that would allow those seeds to grow.

Sometimes as Christ-followers, it seems that our faith is fading. At those times we need to ask God to take the seeds planted in our souls and allow them to grow into strong faith.

I am so thankful for parents who loved God and me enough to faithfully plant seeds of His word and faith in my soul for so many years.

Prayer: Heavenly Father, thank You for the precious seeds of Your word and faith that have been planted in our hearts. Thank You that they have grown into saving faith, and that they continue growing as we walk with You. Help us learn to sow seeds of faith in the lives of those with whom we come in contact. In Jesus' name, Amen.

Thought for the Day: What kinds of seeds are you sowing in the lives of your family, friends, and those whom the Lord brings into your life?

Day 5: Irrevocable Gifts
by Harriet
Read 1 Corinthians 12:4-7, Romans 11:29

For the gifts and the calling of God are irrevocable.
Romans 11:29 (NASB)

My first grandchild, my daughter's son, celebrates a spring birthday. Grason was born six weeks early on a bright spring morning. His birth was not without trauma, including an emergency C-section and then intravenous antibiotics for him and my daughter, both of whom developed serious infections. By God's grace both made full recoveries. As he grew, he delighted us all as we celebrated and treasured his every milestone, with some celebrations larger than others.

The day we celebrated Grason's fourth birthday was supposed to be low key—just family and a couple of his little friends. We had planned to go to a playground and have a picnic lunch, cake, ice cream, and presents.

However, our plans changed when the skies darkened, and it poured down rain. At the last minute, we went to a nearby pizza place instead. This particular pizza restaurant was geared toward children and had a large play area with rides and games. So Grason had a grand party after all, with pizza, cake, presents, balloons, entertainment, and, of course, the ice cream that he loved.

The next morning Grason ran into his mother's room to wake her up and asked excitedly, "Is today still my birthday?"

His mother gently explained that it was not, because his birthday came only once a year and it had been the day before. Though noticeably disappointed, Grason seemed to take the news pretty well. Then they walked into the kitchen together for some breakfast.

When he stepped into the kitchen, Grason looked to his right toward the family room. With eyes lit up, he ran into the family room where all of his opened gifts still sat from the day before. He exclaimed with genuine joyful surprise, "My toys are *still* here, and my balloons too."

My daughter laughed when he did this, and I

laughed when she told me about it. She commented that Grason must have thought everything from the day before would be gone since it was no longer his birthday, including his gifts—as if they had all been rentals.

When I heard this story, I thought about how funny it was that he had thought the gifts we gave him were not his to keep. Then today's Bible verse came to my mind. Do we think this way about the good gifts God gives to us? Perhaps we are this shortsighted when it comes to God's gifts to us.

But like my daughter reassured her son that the gifts she had given him were his to keep, so too our Heavenly Father reassures us in His word that His gifts also are ours to keep. Today's verse tells us in plain words that God's gifts and callings are irrevocable.

Notice that it includes God's calling, too. I had a cousin who felt called to preach as a young man. However, in time, he became frustrated with the church where he served and left the clergy. He spent some years working as a teacher, but in his later years, he returned to the ministry and found himself once again standing in a pulpit on Sunday mornings preaching God's word to a new congregation. God's callings, like His gifts, are irrevocable.

Prayer: Heavenly Father, thank You for the unique gifts and callings You give to each of us. Thank You that we all have a gift and a calling; there is no child of Yours who is empty-handed. And thank You for making those gifts and callings irrevocable. In Jesus' name, Amen.

Thought for the Day: When God gives you a gift, it's yours to keep.

Chapter 7

The Cost of Beauty

Day 1: Lovely Source of True Delight

by Shirley
Read Psalm 37:3-5

Delight yourself in the LORD . . .
Psalm 37:4a

Several years ago, I arrived at the church for a wedding rehearsal, made my way up to the piano to get my music organized, and waited for further instructions from the wedding director. Soon I, and all the others who would be involved in the ceremony, had our instructions and it was time for the rehearsal to begin. As the bride and her father started down the aisle, the bride was telling him to hold her arm differently and to walk slower. Then she was telling the wedding director that the bridesmaids weren't in the right places, and numerous other things. They got to the end of the aisle and stood with the groom standing beside the bride's father. As the preacher explained to the father what he would ask and then how the father would respond, the bride turned around to tell the wedding director about something that needed to be done differently. She didn't even notice that her father had let go of her arm and her groom was standing next to her.

Finally she turned around and the groom said, "Glad you noticed I'm here." We all had a good laugh at that one.

But things were very different the next afternoon, as the doors at the back of the worship center opened and the bride and her father began their walk down the aisle. The piano was turned so I could see them as they came down the aisle. The bride's dress, veil, and train were absolutely gorgeous, and her bouquet was exquisite. But those weren't the things I noticed. Even through her veil I could see that the bride's eyes were fixed on the man to whom her father was giving her. Her love and affection for her husband-to-be radiated through her joyful smile and adoring eyes. She was delighting in him. And this time, she was urging her father to walk faster.

When she and her father were about halfway down the aisle, one of the candelabras on the platform tipped over. The pastor and a groomsman were quick to extinguish the candles so they didn't burn anything. The bride didn't even notice the commotion. I don't think I've ever seen smiles more beautiful than when the groom lifted the bride's veil and she gazed directly into his eyes. Nothing could make her take her eyes off of her beloved. It was so touching to witness.

During the ceremony, the pastor made reference to the excellent example of how our relationship with Jesus Christ should be. He went on to explain that in the same way the bride was eager and hurried to get to her groom, we need to be eager to follow the commands of God. We should love and adore Him so deeply that nothing is able to distract us, so that we take our eyes off of Him.

Remembering this wedding ceremony reminded me of the words of the hymn "Lovely Source of True Delight," by Anne Steele.

> Thou lovely Source of true delight,
> whom I unseen adore,
> unveil Thy beauties to my sight

that I may love Thee more.

Here we sing of Jesus Christ, the Source of salvation, strength, comfort, blessings, and true delight for Christ-followers. We can know and see Him through His word. Our Scripture reading today tells us to delight in the Lord.

The picture of the bride with her veil is a reminder that even though we can know God through His word and see glimpses of Him in creation, we have not actually seen Him in all of His glory. So, in this stanza, we ask God to unveil His beauties.

I found a handwritten note in a file with the words of this hymn that said, "Christ is unveiled as we read, study, memorize, meditate and contemplate upon His word and by His empowerment we live as that word tells us to live and do what it tells us to do." Our knowledge of Him, when understanding is given by the Holy Spirit, propels and compels us to love Him more and serve Him better.

Prayer: Gracious Father, thank You for our

salvation, strength, comfort, and blessings. As we get to know You better through Your word, teach us to delight in You and learn to love You better. In Jesus' name, Amen.

Thought for the Day: When things distract us and our eyes become distracted onto other things, we need to fix our eyes on "Jesus, the founder and perfecter of our faith" (Hebrews 12:2a).

Day 2: God's Treasure

by Harriet
Read Matthew 13:44-46

*The kingdom of heaven is like a merchant
looking for fine pearls.
When he found one of great value,
he went away and sold everything
he had and bought it.*
Matthew 13:45-46 (NIV)

Spring is a time of blossoming beauty. Flowers and green plants spring up from the ground, birds and butterflies begin to flit around, and bunnies and other critters give birth to new life.

All this beauty comes at a cost. The flowers lay buried in the ground as bulbs or seeds before they burst forth and spread open their colorful petals. The birds have to peck open their shells, something that is pretty exhausting to tiny hatchlings. The butterflies break out of their cocoons finally leaving their old lives as caterpillars completely behind. You get the picture—beauty usually has a cost.

Many years ago in an adult Bible study, we

studied the parable of the treasure in the field, and the pearl of great price—the stories Jesus told in today's devotional reading. In these two parables, Jesus makes the same point: a man finds a treasure of some kind and values it so much that he sells everything he has to gain it.

I've always been able to relate to this story, at least part of it. As a child, the Nigerian ground around me sometimes held treasures just waiting to be discovered. Where I lived, the treasures were mostly in the form of quartz crystals and shiny pieces of mica that glistened brightly when illuminated by the sun. But if we traveled up north, other treasures could be discovered. There were places in northern Nigeria where semiprecious stones like amethysts and tourmalines were not too hard to find laying on the ground if one looked hard enough. I remember being told that even precious stones, such as rubies could sometimes be found in those areas north of my town of Ogbomoso. To my knowledge, though, none of my friends ever found a ruby. Amethysts and tourmalines were a different story, and many of my friends found those. My treasure hunting success stayed limited to quartz crystals, which fascinated me just the same.

The Bible does not identify the treasure that the man found in that field. As a child, I always imagined that it was a giant ruby, beautiful beyond words, and immensely valuable. But that man's beautiful treasure had a cost. He had to sell everything in order to purchase the field. This the man did, not only willingly but also eagerly, because the treasure was worth that much, literally everything, to him.

I have heard this parable all my life. I always assumed the man in the parable was me, or any other human who discovered Jesus for the first time. We want the eternal salvation that Jesus offers through His death on the cross so badly that we are willing to give up everything to follow Christ.

There are ample verses that validate this interpretation, such as when the apostles gave up everything to follow Jesus, and verses like Luke 14:33 where Jesus said, ". . . those of you who do not give up everything you have cannot be my disciples" (NIV) and Mark 8:35, "For whoever wants to save their life will lose it, but whoever loses their life for me and for the gospel will save it" (NIV).

Yet, that is not the only valid interpretation. That year in adult Bible study I learned another interpretation I had never pondered before—that the person finding the treasure and giving up everything in this parable is Jesus, and the treasure He found is me . . . and you. This interpretation is verified by Scripture as well, in that Jesus left His throne in heaven and allowed Himself to be nailed to a cross to purchase us with His very blood.

Now when I read this story, I picture Jesus walking that field scanning the ground with His eyes, the way I used to scan the Nigerian ground, searching for His lost treasure—souls for whom He died. What a precious thought.

Prayer: Gracious Heavenly Father, thank You for claiming us as Your treasure and providing a way of salvation for us. May we never take Your gift of salvation for granted. In Jesus' name, Amen.

Thought for the Day: Jesus gave up everything for us.

Day 3: A Costly Love
by Shirley
Read Mark 15:33-39

"My God, my God, why have you forsaken me?"
Mark 15:34b

Today we are going to look at the love of God that saved us through His Son Jesus, who died on a cross to purchase our salvation. The following passage reminds us that it is by God's grace alone that we are saved; we didn't do anything to earn it. "For by grace you have been saved through faith. And this is not your own doing; it is the gift of God, not a result of works, so that no one may boast" (Ephesians 2:8-9).

The gift of salvation is freely given to us by God (Romans 3:24). There is nothing that any of us can do to earn our salvation. Salvation was free to us and salvation was very costly for Jesus. When thinking of what salvation cost Jesus, we often do not think about the fact that He left heaven in all of its glory to take on human form and live on earth. Before He was crucified, Jesus was mocked and beaten, even though He had lived a sinless life. Jesus experienced excruciating pain as He was raised up and hung on the cross to die as payment for our sins, and He experienced the wrath of God because our sins were laid on Him. Our key passage shows us that the horrendous consequence of our sin is separation from God, when Jesus on the cross says, "My God, My God, why have you forsaken me?"

The free gift of salvation we receive from God through His Son Jesus was bought at a very high price so that we could become His children (John 1:12). Because He loves us, Jesus, the Son of God, chose to lay down His life for us as "a fragrant offering and sacrifice to God" (Ephesians 5:2).

Frances Ridley Havergal's hymn, "I Gave My Life for Thee," clearly explains God's costly and beautiful love:

> I gave My life for thee;
> My precious blood I shed
> that thou might'st ransomed be

and quickened from the dead.
I gave, I gave My life for thee;
what hast thou giv'n for Me?

My Father's house of light—
My glory circled throne—
I left for earthly night,
for wanderings sad and lone.
I left, I left it all for thee;
hast thou left aught (anything) for Me?

I suffered much for thee—
more than thy tongue can tell
of bitt'rest agony—
to rescue thee from hell.
I've borne, I've borne it all for thee;
what hast thou borne for Me?

And I have brought to thee,
down from My home above,
salvation full and free,
My pardon and My love.
I bring, I bring rich gifts to thee;
what hast thou brought to Me?

Each stanza presents something God has done for us and challenges us with a question that guides us in understanding how we are to respond to the costly and beautiful love of Christ for us—with gratefulness.

- "I [Christ] gave My life for you . . . What have you given for Me?" We are to give ourselves to Him as a living sacrifice (Romans 12:1), and give Him our sacrifices of worship by living lives that glorify Him (1 Peter 2:5-6).
- "I [Christ] left everything, my Father and the glory of heaven . . . Have you left everything behind?" In Luke 14:33, Jesus says, ". . . any one of you who does not renounce all that he has cannot be my disciple."
- "I [Christ] endured excruciating pain for you . . . What have you endured for me?" As Christ-followers we are smack in the middle of a struggle against evil that manifests itself in our hardships, trouble, and sometimes persecution. We are called to steadfastly endure trials (James 1:12).
- "I [Christ] gave you rich gifts of salvation,

pardon, and love ... What have you given me?" We are to love God with every fiber of our being so that He is glorified in everything we do and say (Matthew 22:37).

How in the world is it possible for us to do these things? We allow God's love to completely transform us and grow deep roots within us as we live for Him. Part of Paul's testimony, found in Galatians 2:20, was ". . . the life I now live in the flesh I live by faith in the Son of God, who loved me and gave himself for me." As Christ-followers, Jesus calls us to be busy working for our Father as we live our lives to glorify Him.

Prayer: Heavenly Father, thank You for Your beautiful love that gave us life eternal, as well as provision to live here on earth. May we gratefully respond to Your love by giving ourselves totally to You, leaving everything behind, by steadfastly enduring hardships, trouble, and persecution, and by loving You with every fiber of our being. In Jesus' name we pray, Amen.

Thought for the Day: In view of Christ's costly and beautiful love, ". . . what have any of us to lose for Jesus compared with what we gain by him?" – Charles Spurgeon

Day 4: Real Beauty

by Harriet
Read 1 Peter 3:3-4

Charm is deceptive, and beauty is fleeting;
but a woman who fears the LORD is to be praised.
Proverbs 31:30 (NIV)

I am female, and like most females, I place some value on beauty, perhaps more than I should. It's a thin line we Christian women walk between striving for beauty as the world presents it and not striving so much that it is inappropriate.

Women are naturally beautiful and beautifying creatures. We beautify everything around us. It's an instinct God gave us. I read recently of a study that concluded that a messy room bothers females more than it does males. As a wife of one husband and the mother of three sons, I can certainly affirm these results. They could have just asked me and saved all the money and effort they put into that study. The males in my life can sit and watch a ball game no matter the condition of the room around them, but if there are dishes in the sink or items strewn on the floor, I have trouble ignoring them. I feel driven to pick up and clean up or in other words . . . beautify the world around me.

My grandson once commented on my daughter's desire for a clean house when he told me, "My mother loves to clean. She cleans all the time because she loves it so much." I couldn't help but remember the messy little girl who used to live at my house. Even she somehow morphed into a hardworking woman who apparently works so constantly at keeping her home clean that her son thinks it's an activity she enjoys and does for pleasure.

We women often work just as hard at beautifying ourselves—our bodies and faces. And talk about the cost of beauty. There is no limit to the amount of money a person, male or female, could pay to make changes in their faces or bodies that they consider improvements. Usually though, they are actually only conforming themselves to the current standard of beauty as the fashion of the day dictates.

Real beauty is not made from these practices.

It is not made from keeping a clean house or wearing the latest makeup or clothing. Think for a minute of the people you know, personally or otherwise. Often people seem attractive, even beautiful, until you get to know them better—who they really are, what they stand for.

I knew a woman once whom the world considered beautiful. She had a small, slim figure and lovely facial features. But when I got to know her better, she quickly became someone I tried to avoid. Likewise I once knew a man who appeared handsome, but I heard from his daughter that he actually had a violent temper which he often inflicted on his wife and daughters. This man never seemed handsome to me again after finding that out.

What does the Bible say about real beauty? In 1 Samuel 16:7 we learn the Lord does not consider appearance or physical features like height because God does not look at the kinds of things people do. God looks at the heart instead. This passage was a recording of what the prophet said when he was searching for the new king that he was to anoint. That king ended up being David, whom we know had a beautiful heart, because in I Samuel 13:14, God said he was a man after God's own heart.

A beautiful heart is one that loves God as well as one's fellow man. The best description of the kind of heart God searches for is found in Luke 10:27, in what Jesus identified as the greatest commandment: "Love the Lord your God with all your heart and with all your soul and with all your strength and with all your mind, and love your neighbor as yourself" (NIV). This is real beauty.

Prayer: Father, in this world we so often become confused as to what real beauty looks like. As humans we naturally look to the physical world for what our eyes perceive as lovely, whether that be in people or places. Your eyes differ from ours. You see hearts. We cannot see hearts, but we can glimpse them as we see actions. Help us to learn to place value on what You value. In Jesus' name, Amen.

Thought for the Day: Can you think of someone who is beautiful because of the way they show their love for God and their fellow man?

Day 5: Beautiful Fountain of Blood

by Shirley
Read Hebrews 9:11-22

*Indeed, under the law almost everything
is purified with blood,
and without the shedding of blood
there is no forgiveness of sins.*
Hebrews 9:22

Many years ago, I took a friend to the doctor for some tests. Since I knew we would be there several hours, I took my laptop with me so I could work on finishing my notes for the Sunday school lesson I would teach the Sunday before Easter. I was apparently humming a hymn, because a lady sitting directly across from me asked what I was humming.

I said, ""There is a Fountain." It's a hymn about how we can be saved through the shed blood of Jesus Christ. Do you know it?"

With an incredulous look on her face she said, "Of course I do, but we don't sing that at my church. I just don't see any reason to sing about blood. That's just not a suitable subject for a church service. Why, if we sang about blood some people might not ever come back."

I was so stunned that I didn't speak again for a minute or so. I asked the Lord to guard my tongue to speak the truth in love, and said, "So what will you sing this Sunday and at your Good Friday service, if you have one?"

She replied, "Oh, you know, the regular Good Friday and Easter stuff," and she named several that basically talk about how much God loves us.

We continued our conversation for the next few minutes. Sadly, I don't think she ever understood the importance of singing about the blood of Jesus. I still can't understand how in the world you can have a Good Friday service and not talk about the shed blood of Christ that atoned for our sins.

Admittedly, to an unbeliever who does not know God or the Bible, it likely is strange to hear people singing about blood as precious, cleansing, and powerful. For some, the thought of blood conjures up all sorts of mental images that are not pleasant. However, without the shed blood of Jesus Christ, there was not a cross. Without the cross, Christ was not resurrected from the dead. Without the resurrection, we are without any real hope.

There are many beautiful hymns about the blood of Jesus. Written by William Cowper, "There is a Fountain," accentuates the significance of the blood of Jesus Christ in our salvation, for blood has always been necessary for the remission of our sin, as we read in today's key passage.

> There is a fountain filled with blood
> drawn from Immanuel's veins,
> and sinners plunged beneath that flood
> lose all their guilty stains . . . .

This fountain is filled with blood that came from the veins of Immanuel—God with us. Sinners are forgiven when they plunge into the blood; they are cleansed of their sins because of the redemption that comes through the blood of Jesus Christ.

> The dying thief rejoiced to see
> that fountain in His day.

And there have I, though vile as he,
Washed all my sins away . . . .

In the same way that the thief on the cross beside Jesus was saved, we can be saved also. Every sin we commit is an insult to holy God. "For all have sinned and fall short of the glory of God" (Romans 3:23). Because of the shed blood of Jesus, our sin can be washed away.

Dear dying Lamb, Thy precious blood
shall never lose its pow'r,
till all the ransomed church of God
Are safe, to sin no more . . . .

John called Jesus ". . . the Lamb of God, who takes away the sin of the world" (John 1:29). Then in 1 Peter, we read that we are ransomed "with the precious blood of Christ, like that of a lamb without blemish or spot" (1 Peter 1:19). The blood of Jesus Christ will never lose its power to save, as those who have been saved on earth will be saved for eternity in heaven where they will sin no more.

E'er since by faith I saw the stream
Thy flowing wounds supply,
redeeming love has been my theme
and shall be till I die . . . .

It is only by faith that we can see the stream of blood that Christ's bleeding wounds supply, and through which we are saved. Christ's blood and the blessings it brings come to us because of God's redeeming love that sent Jesus to save us (John 3:16). So, our music or topic or focus from now until we die is Jesus Christ and Him crucified (1 Corinthians 2:2).

When this poor, lisping, stamm'ring tongue
Lies silent in the grave,
Then in a nobler, sweeter song,
I'll sing Thy pow'r to save ....

We have just sung that God's redeeming love will be the focus of our life, "And shall be till I die." Now, in a song that is nobler and sweeter than we are able to sing here on earth, we sing about what will happen when we die. Then, we will continue to sing in heaven of God's redeeming love and His power to save.

While to some singing about Jesus' blood is gross, to a Christ-follower it is a song of praise and thanksgiving for the precious blood of Jesus that atoned for our sin. It is a beautiful fountain of blood that is supplied by the veins of Jesus Christ bringing redemption and justification to us because of God's redeeming love.

Prayer: Heavenly Father, thank You for the fountain of blood that You provided through Jesus that cleanses my sin and saves me to live here on earth and for eternity with You. May we ever remember the sacrifice Christ paid on the cross. In Jesus' name, Amen.

Thought for the Day: By God's mercy and grace, through the beautiful fountain of Jesus' blood we can be forgiven of our sin, regardless of how great and horrendous that sin may be.

Chapter 8

Hang in there; Sunday's Coming

Day 1: Palm Sunday
by Harriet
Read Revelation 7:9-10

They took palm branches and
went out to meet him, shouting,
"Hosanna! Blessed is he who comes
in the name of the Lord!"
John 12:13a (NIV)

Palm Sunday is the day when Christians everywhere remember Jesus' triumphant entry into Jerusalem. He rode into Jerusalem on a donkey and was celebrated by a mass of people who waved palm branches at Him and shouted, "Hosanna! Blessed is he who comes in the name of the Lord!"

I love palm branches. My childhood home was a place filled with palm trees. We had tall, stately palm trees that dotted our beautiful horizons and small, compact ones which we often used in landscaping to decorate our yards. When I first came back to America, the beautiful wispy palm branches waving in the breeze and the tall, thin, stately palm trees standing at attention seemingly everywhere was one of the things I missed most.

As a child, I and my friends often played with palm branches. One of the Bible stories we loved to act out was the story of the triumphant entry. At church the students in my Sunday school class were given branches to wave while my mother told the Bible story in the Yoruba language. I did not understand much of what my mother, said, but I loved standing next to my happy Nigerian friends waving branches at an imaginary Jesus riding past us on a donkey.

There is another place in Scripture that tells about a crowd of people waving palm branches. In this scene found in Revelation 7:9-10, the apostle John describes his vision. He says he saw a great multitude of people from every nation, tribe, and language, so large they could not be numbered. These people stood before the throne of God clothed in white robes with palm branches in their hands and proclaimed in loud voices that salvation belongs to God who sits on the throne and to the Lamb of God.

This crowd is very different from the one in

Jerusalem that waved palm branches at Jesus riding past them on a donkey. The crowd in Jerusalem was a fickle bunch. Just a week after they treated him so affectionately, this same crowd stood *en masse* shouting again. But this time, instead of shouting "Hosanna" at Jesus, they shout, "Crucify Him." Instead of praising Jesus, they sought His death. In contrast, the crowd we read about in Revelation is made up of true believers praising God for their salvation.

Some years ago, I was privileged to hear Steve Saint speak. He is the son of Nate Saint, the missionary to Ecuador who was martyred along with several other missionaries in January of 1956. I was a substitute teacher at a Christian school, and we had Steve Saint as a chapel speaker about the time the movie *The End of the Spear* was released. What a blessing I received. I recall Steve Saint saying that this verse drove his father and the other brave missionaries to push ahead with their evangelistic efforts to the very tribe that ended up killing them. The tribe was unreached and had a language understood by few. Steve said his father and the other missionaries kept saying that if people of every nation and language will someday stand in front of God's throne praising Him, then the people of that rare, unknown tribal tongue needed to be reached with the gospel, too.

What a difference in those two crowds of people. The Revelation group truly understood who Jesus was and the sacrifice He made for them. They understood that Jesus was God making Himself a man, descending to earth to pay the sacrifice for their sin . . . for our sin.

And who are these people gathered around the throne? Everyone who accepts the sacrifice Jesus made on the cross. Christianity is not offered to only a select few. It is offered freely to all people of all nations—every kindred, tribe, and tongue. Today we know that the people Nate Saint and those other missionaries died trying to reach will be in that throng before God's throne. They will stand alongside me and Christians from my nation who speak my tongue, and alongside Christian Nigerians whose tongue I could not speak but my mother could. Palm Sunday always brings this crowd to my mind.

Prayer: Lord, there is such a contrast in these two

palm-waving crowds. May we search our hearts and gain understanding concerning to which crowd we truly belong. If anyone reading this book does not fully understand the salvation You offer, guide the reader to a better understanding of Your saving grace. In Jesus' name, Amen.

Thought for the Day: To which crowd do you belong?

Day 2: Extraordinary Humility

by Shirley
Read John 13:1-10

A new commandment I give to you,
that you love one another:
just as I have loved you,
you also are to love one another.
John 13:34

For many Christ-followers, Palm Sunday and Good Friday observances prepare our hearts and lead us into our Easter celebrations. Between Palm Sunday and Good Friday comes Maundy Thursday, although many do not know what it is all about.

Maundy Thursday is observed the Thursday before Easter. It is remembered as the day when Jesus and His disciples shared the Passover meal. Maundy means "command," referring to the new command that Jesus gave to the disciples.

Today's reading tells us that Jesus knew it was time for Him to be crucified, and that Judas was ready to betray him, so He was instructing the disciples how to live and love others.

Verses 3-5 of this passage tell us that Jesus took off His outer garment, tied a towel around His waist, poured water into a basin, and began washing the feet of His disciples. He then dried them with the towel He had around His waist.

Let's dig a little deeper into what all happened here. Foot-washing seems like a weird practice to most of us, but it was a common hospitality practice in the days of Jesus. Remember, they didn't have paved roads and vehicles to transport them from place to place. They wore sandals probably made of leather and rope and they had to walk on dirt roads, so their feet were generally pretty filthy. The first thing they would do when they arrived at someone's tent or house was to wash off their feet from the dust and grime of the journey. In most homes, guests were provided water and towels so they could wash their own feet. In the homes of the richer people, a slave of the house would wash and dry one's feet. Even in the ordinary houses, a household member or servant would wash the feet of those who were guests of honor, giving them extra respect. The foot washing not only ensured the guests had clean feet, but it would refresh them as well.

Jesus washing the feet of the disciples would have been a very big deal. He was an important person, the guest of honor, at least well enough known that crowds gathered around and followed Him wherever He went. Are you getting the picture here? Jesus, the Son of God—who has all power and authority in heaven and on earth—in humility, took on the role of a slave and washed the feet of each disciple as an example of true humility and love.

To put it deeper into perspective, remember that, not long before this, the disciples had been arguing about who was the greatest. Obviously, the disciples had not heeded His teaching that the first must be last and serve everyone (Mark 9:33-35). Contrast the extraordinary humility of Christ as He washed the feet of the disciples to the disciples vying for seats of honor in glory.

After washing their feet, Jesus took off the towel and put His outer garment back on. Then He asked them, "Do you understand what I have done for you?" (John 13:12)

Matthew Henry gives four reasons why Christ washed the feet of the disciples. They include to "testify His love to the disciples," as an example of "humility and condescension," to "signify to them spiritual washing," and to "set them an example."

As Christ showed His love for the disciples, He was setting the groundwork for the commandment He would give them: "A new commandment I give to you, that you love one another: just as I have loved you, you also are to love one another" (John 13:34).

I'm not sure that any of us will have this kind of love except perhaps in small intermittent quantities. Why? Because God's love for us is ultimate love. It is self-sacrificing—He gave Himself for us because He loved us. It's a high standard to meet. So many times we are so self-absorbed that we are not even aware of those around us who could use some loving interaction.

Jesus goes on to say, "By this all people will know that you are my disciples, if you have love for one another" (John 13:35). Oh my. I am certain that there are times when people do not know I am a Christ-follower because of the way they observe me not loving others.

It often takes humility to love others. When we truly love God, which means we obey His commands (John 14:15), we have the strength and desire to love others in the way Jesus taught and showed us to love.

Prayer: Heavenly Father, thank You for the way You showed us to serve one another. Help me remember that without Your cleansing, I would be lost and without hope. Forgive me for not loving others. Help me learn to love others as You love them. In the name of Jesus, Amen.

Thought for the Day: In what ways is God calling you to humbly serve others?

Day 3: Don't Cry
by Harriet
Read 1 Corinthians 15:53-57

Precious in the sight of the LORD
is the death of his faithful servants.
Psalm 116:15 (NIV)

Reverend Adediran was a pastor for thirty years when he retired and moved back to his home city of Ogbomoso. But after his retirement, another church in his city needed a pastor and asked Rev. Adediran if he would lead them. After prayerful consideration, he agreed to assume the pastorate at Oke Lerin Baptist Church in Ogbomoso, Nigeria. The members of Oke Lerin got a bargain when they hired Rev. Adediran. They were able to pay him less money than they would have paid another pastor because, after all, Rev. Adediran was retired. Retired or not, he served at Oke Lerin faithfully—for another twenty-nine years. Altogether, he pastored for fifty-nine years, only serving two churches—thirty years at one and twenty-nine more at another as a "retired, interim" pastor.

With the passing of time, he and his wife grew older and her health began to fail. Then one day Mrs. Adediran became quite sick and died. The news spread quickly throughout the city. They were both much loved by the people there. She had been a kind and gentle woman and all who knew her suffered a great loss. My parents were among those who knew and loved the Adedirans and who attended her funeral.

My parents approached the church slowly and reverently, making their way past the crowd that had gathered outside, into the little church building also filled with people. People sat on the pews and others stood around in small groups talking amongst themselves quietly. The crowd included church members as well as other people. Many townspeople who did not attend the church came to pay their respects as well.

My mother began to cry as she entered the church, grieving the passing of her dear friend. Rev. Adediran stood in the front of the church, greeting those who had come. When he spotted my parents from across the room and saw my mother's tears, he hurried over with a sense of urgency about him. With noticeable concern in his voice, Rev, Adediran spoke in a quiet but firm tone to my tearful mother as he instructed her, "My sister, do not cry. You must not cry. The people will see you."

His words surprised my mother, until he explained further, "There are some here who are not believers, and they will not understand. We have told them death is different for believers. We have preached hope to them. We have a hope that they do not have. My wife is in a better place. She is with her Savior. You and I know that is true, but if the people here who do not know Jesus see your tears, they will be confused. They will think we do not truly believe what we have said to them. They will think we have no hope."

Rev. Adediran's words pierced deeply into my mother's heart. In the American culture in which she grew up, it was customary to cry at the passing of a friend or loved one, shedding tears because of the personal loss one naturally feels. But she also knew that he was correct in his point of view. A believer who passes from this earth is with the Lord—the risen Lord.

Life can be difficult at times. Days of sadness and uncertainty can drag on. The days between Good Friday and Easter Sunday were some of those uncertain times for the disciples. They had believed in and followed Jesus at great personal cost and then they had watched Him be nailed to a cross and buried. Their faith must have wavered both personally and collectively as doubts set in. Like my mother when her dear friend died, they must have been filled with sadness.

But Sunday was coming . . .

Hold on to your faith in times of sadness and doubt. As Rev. Adediran would say, others are watching to see if we really believe what we claim to believe.

Prayer: Heavenly Father, we turn to You when fear and sadness grip us. Wrap us in Your love during these times and grow our faith. In Jesus' name, Amen.

Thought for the Day: God understands our fear and sadness. Hang in there, Sunday's coming.

Day 4: At Calvary

by Shirley
Read 1 Timothy 1:12-17

*. . . But I received mercy because
I had acted ignorantly in unbelief,
and the grace of our Lord overflowed for me
with the faith and love that are in Christ Jesus.*
1 Timothy 1:13b-14

Good Friday is one of my many favorite worship services each year. It is a somber remembrance of the crucifixion of Christ. We leave the Good Friday service, and Jesus is dead in the tomb. Back during the time these events were actually unfolding, I imagine the devil and demons were having a great big celebration, don't you? Since we live now and have the Bible, we know that the devil did not win because the Son rose on Sunday.

We sometimes want to hastily pass by the cross to get to the jubilation of the resurrection on Sunday. Instead of rushing past the cross, though, let's look at it carefully. Jesus came to earth as fully God and fully man. Philippians 2:8 tells us, "Being found in human form, he humbled himself by becoming obedient to the point of death, even death on a cross." Contemplating the cross helps us better understand the all-powerful servant God we worship.

As we contemplate the agony and suffering of Jesus on the cross—what our sin cost Him—we begin to realize the depth of our sin and repent. This realization results in a deeper desire to know Him better and to glorify Him in and through everything we say and do.

Contemplating the cross helps us gain a deeper understanding of the depth of God's love for us, thus compelling us to love Him more and obey His commands.

By contemplating the cross, we see the example Christ set of how we are to live as those empowered by the Holy Spirit to humbly serve our God and others.

As Good Friday has us pondering the sacrifice of Christ on the cross, the hymn "At Calvary," by William R. Newell comes to mind.

Years I spent in vanity and pride
caring not my Lord was crucified,
knowing not it was for me He died
on Calvary.

In this stanza we learn that Jesus died on Calvary, on the cross, for our sins. In today's Scripture reading, the Apostle Paul tells us that before Christ saved him, he was "a blasphemer, persecutor, and insolent opponent" (1 Timothy 1:13a). Before we came to Christ, we may not have sinned in the ways Paul did, but our sin was also great. We also didn't know or care that Jesus died for us.

Refrain:
Mercy there was great, and grace was free.
Pardon there was multiplied to me.
There my burdened soul found liberty
at Calvary.

The refrain gives us opportunity to express our joy and thanksgiving for the mercy and grace that God extended to us at Calvary. I've heard mercy described as not getting what we deserve for our sin. Titus 3:4-5 speaks of God's mercy: "But when the goodness and kindness of God appeared, He saved us, not because of works done by us in righteousness, but according to his own mercy; by the washing of regeneration and renewal of the Holy Spirit."

At Calvary, God's grace extended the channel of salvation through the shed blood of Christ. Ephesians 2:8 tells us that we have been saved by grace through faith—a gift from God.

As we continue singing, we are reminded that without the law, we would not recognize sin (Romans 7:7-9). The law puts a spotlight on our sin, and the Holy Spirit convicts us of that sin so that we can repent and seek forgiveness from God. Salvation comes when we turn to Calvary.

Another stanza pleads Christ-followers to give Jesus everything, which will show we recognize that He is our King. Then our redeemed soul can sing praises and thanksgiving for Calvary.

O the love that drew salvation's plan!

O the grace that brought it down to man!
O the mighty gulf that God did span
at Calvary!

In the final stanza we contemplate the love and grace that God showed us through the finished work of Christ at Calvary. God's love drew the plan for salvation. God's mercy, in the form of Jesus Christ, brought that plan down to us and bridged the "mighty gulf" that separated us from God.

While the emphasis of this hymn is the saving mercy of God at Calvary, don't miss the point that once we become Christ-followers, it is because of Calvary that we have empowerment to live our lives glorifying God. Contemplating Calvary renews our love and passion for, and gratitude to, Jesus Christ and His finished work on the cross.

Prayer: Heavenly Father, thank You for Your mercy, grace, and love You poured out on us through Calvary. Give us a passion to draw closer to You and be obedient to Your commands. In Jesus' name, Amen.

Thought for the Day: "Love so amazing, so

divine, demands my soul, my life, my all." – Isaac Watts, *When I Survey the Wondrous Cross*

Day 5: Gethsemane

by Harriet
Read Matthew 26:36-39

We are hard pressed on every side, but not crushed;
perplexed, but not in despair;
persecuted, but not abandoned;
struck down, but not destroyed.
2 Corinthians 4:8-9 (NIV)

The garden of Gethsemane, where Jesus prayed the night he was arrested, lies at the foot of the Mount of Olives just outside of Jerusalem. The word Gethsemane comes from the two Hebrew words, *geth,* which means press and *shemen,* which means oil.

The process used to extract olive oil back in Jesus' day had two parts. First, whole olives were put into a stone basin with a millstone placed on them. Then a horse or donkey was harnessed and led around in a circular motion, causing the millstone to roll over the olives many times, cracking them. The cracked olives were then put into a burlap bag and placed under a large stone column called a gethsemane. The enormous weight of the column squeezed the olives, causing the precious oil to run out, allowing it to be collected.

While Jesus was in the garden of Gethsemane, otherwise known as the garden of the olive press, He too felt an enormous burden crushing down on Him. Unlike the olives, Jesus' burden was not a physical one. He bore a heavy emotional and spiritual burden instead. Yet, what did He say? Matthew 26:39 tells us that after pleading with God to take the burden from Him, He said, "Yet, not as I will, but as you will" (NIV). And then what did He do? He went willingly to the cross to gain salvation for you and for me.

In some ways He had been prepared for his personal Gethsemane on his way to the garden that night. The Scripture says Jesus walked through the Kidron Valley to get to Gethsemane. The Hebrew word *Kidron* means dark or black. This particular valley derived its name from the fact that the ground in this valley was dark, even black in color. Why was the ground black? The temple sat on the hill directly above it. When the priests practiced animal sacrifice, their blood ran out of the temple, down the hill, and into the Kidron Valley, turning the ground black as it dried.

It amazes me to realize that Jesus passed through this valley on his way to the cross. I wonder what went through His mind as Jesus, the Lamb of God, stepped on the ground that had been made black from the blood of many lambs sacrificed on the hill above it. Maybe He thought of the ordeal He was about to face. Did He agonize as He walked? Certainly He agonized as He prayed in the garden.

I ponder these things at Easter time. Did He look into the future and see my face, or yours? Jesus gave His life for us. What have we given Him today?

Are you in your own Gethsemane right now? What is crushing down on you? When the olives were crushed, out came the precious, treasured oil. When Jesus was crushed, from His blood came our salvation. Look for the good things God will bring about in your time of trial.

Prayer: Heavenly Father, help us to hold on to

You in our times of trial, when we feel pressure crushing in on us from all sides. Help us to yield to Your will, like Jesus did in the garden. And help us to see the good You are bringing out of it all. In Jesus' name, Amen.

Thought for the Day: God brings good from all things.

Chapter 9

Celebrate the Resurrection

Day 1: Have You Heard the Good News?

by Shirley
Read Matthew 28:18-20

"O death, where is your victory?
O death, where is your sting?"
1 Corinthians 15:55

Anyone who has heard me teach or talk about the joy of the Lord knows that I use my mom as my quintessential earthly example of one who consistently radiated the joy of the Lord. When that barely five-foot-tall, gray-headed grandmother walked into a room, she lit it up. For full disclosure, you need to know that Mom was probably also dancing or kicking up her heels (literally) as she entered.

Although Mom was energetic and fun loving, that isn't what you first noticed about her. When she walked in, you immediately noticed her smile and the way her eyes sparkled. She exuded the joy of the Lord—her Lord. People were drawn to her and wanted to know her.

This joy was especially evident in the weeks leading up to Easter as Mom greeted everyone with whom she came in contact, including complete strangers, with a joyful and excited question: "Did you hear the Good News?"

Most people would give her a puzzled look and say, "No, what news?"

I presume they expected some news about Mom winning the lottery, or coming into an inheritance, or something similar.

Mom's response to the question was quick and enthusiastic, and almost always caught the person off guard. She would excitedly answer, "He has risen!"

If the person did not respond in a manner that led Mom to think they understood and knew who He is and why it is such good news that "He is risen," she would begin sharing the gospel with them.

It didn't matter if she was in the parking lot, restroom, grocery store check-out line, hair salon, or anywhere else, Mom made sure that everyone with whom she came in contact heard the good news of the gospel.

Now I realize that everyone doesn't have the type of personality Mom had, so everyone isn't comfortable going up to total strangers and saying anything. Her personality was the mechanism through which she shared the gospel. However, it wasn't Mom's personality that enabled her to go up to total strangers and tell them about Jesus.

Mom was able to tell total strangers about Jesus because of two primary reasons.

First, Jesus Christ redeemed my mom and forgave her sin when she was young. Mom was so grateful for the grace of God that saved her and sustained her throughout her life that she wanted to tell everyone about Him and how to have a relationship with Him.

Second, Mom took Jesus' command in today's passage seriously. She understood this meant she was to talk about Jesus to everyone—non-Christ-follower and Christ-follower alike, obeying her Savior's *Great Commission*.

It also meant that she not only taught those around her about Jesus and what the Bible said we are to do, she showed them how to live a life in obedience to Christ's commands.

And how could she not be excited about the truth that Jesus Christ did not stay dead in the grave but arose victoriously? And how can we not?

Another great hymn comes to mind: "Christ Arose," by Robert Lowry. The first two stanzas are sung quietly and somberly as they speak of Jesus being "low in the grave" and of Jesus in his "bed" or grave when the people seal him in that grave.

After each stanza we sing the triumphant chorus:

Up from the grave he arose
with a mighty triumph o'er his foes.
He arose a victor from the dark domain,
and he lives forever, with His saints to reign.
He arose! He arose! Hallelujah, Christ arose!

The final stanza is my favorite. It begins with the same quiet and somber tone of the first two stanzas as we sing, "Death cannot keep its prey, Jesus my Savior." And then more triumphantly we sing, "He tore the bars away, Jesus my Lord."

As we sing the final chorus, I am reminded of Luke 24:1-7 when the women came to the tomb to prepare Jesus' body with spices and ointments. They found the stone rolled away from the entrance of the tomb, and when they went into the tomb, it was empty. The angels appeared to them and told them, "[Jesus] is not here, but has risen" (verse 6).

Do you remember what happens next? The women go and tell the disciples, who ran to inspect the tomb for themselves because they did not believe the women.

Our grateful response each time we think about Christ rising from the dead should be to thank God for the death, burial, and resurrection of His Son who made atonement for our sin, thus securing our eternal salvation.

We should also be propelled by our gratefulness to proclaim to one and all the Good News my mom loved to proclaim, "He is risen. He is risen, indeed."

Prayer: Heavenly Father, thank You for the death, burial, and resurrection of Your Son Jesus, and for the salvation He bought for us. Thank You that because of our relationship with You through Your Son, we have grace and mercy to walk through our lives victoriously in Your strength. Help us better understand what it means that "Christ rose from the grave." In Jesus' name we pray, Amen.

Thought for the Day: In what ways does the resurrection of Christ compel and propel you to proclaim the Good News that He is risen?

Day 2: By Many or By Few

by Harriet
Read 1 Samuel 14:1-7

*Then Jonathan said to the young man,
who was carrying his armor,
"Come and let us cross over
to the garrison of these uncircumcised;
perhaps the LORD will work for us,
for the LORD is not restrained to save
by many or by few."*
1 Samuel 14:6 (NASB)

On that first Easter morning so long ago, Jesus burst forth from the grave, conquering death for all eternity. Satan and all his efforts to beat Jesus failed. Even Satan's strongest weapon—death—could not keep Jesus down, giving us reason to celebrate.

Our salvation would not be complete if the grave had held Jesus, but it did not, and through His resurrection, Jesus became the victor over death, securing our salvation. Through the sacrifice of one man, many received their salvation. God can work through many, through few, or even alone, if the circumstances require it.

At Easter time we celebrate Jesus' amazing victory over sin and death. The beautiful spring world around us is not our only reason to rejoice. Our hearts leap with the realization of what these biblical truths mean to us. God is stronger than His enemy and through Him we can also overcome the evil one.

Have you ever felt alone? Has God ever given you a task, but seemingly no one to help you accomplish it? In today's passage King Saul's son, Jonathan, attempted a solo military mission accompanied only by his armor bearer. These two brave men attempted to conquer their enemy alone—only themselves and God. It must have felt daunting, but conquer they did. God handed a victory to the Israelites that day using just two men whose faith was great.

Growing up, I often heard my father say, "One with the Lord is a majority." My father was right. One with the Lord certainly is a majority. In fact, the Lord by Himself is a majority even if none should follow Him. Job acknowledged this truth when he said in Job 42:2, "I know that you can do all things, no purpose of yours can be thwarted" (NIV). In Isaiah 63:5, God illustrates this truth when He says, "I looked, but there was no one to help, I was appalled that no one gave support; so my own arm achieved salvation for me" (NIV). And of course, Jesus' resurrection from the grave proves it.

Have you felt God nudging you about anything? What is God speaking to you about today? What is He asking you to do? Rejoice in whatever direction the Lord is leading you. And if in doing what God has called you to do, you find yourself standing alone, remember the truth of Jonathan's words. Nothing can keep the Lord from doing His work—whether by many, by few, or by one.

Prayer: Heavenly Father, we thank You for Easter and all it means for us, now in this life and forever in eternity. Because of Easter, we know we, too, will live again even after we take our last breath in our physical body. Thank You, too, that we are not alone, even when it sometimes seems that way to us. Thank you for strengthening us and enabling us to do whatever it is You have asked of us. In Jesus' name, Amen.

Thought for the Day: God is able. So, stand firm because you are not alone. The God who created you and called you for His purposes will accomplish what He has planned—whether by many, by few, or by one.

Day 3: Cute Mix-ups or Deep Theological Truths?

by Shirley
Read Isaiah 53:3-6

But the angel said to the women, "Do not be afraid,
for I know that you seek Jesus who was crucified.
He is not here, for he has risen, as he said.
Come, see the place where he lay.
Matthew 28:5-6

Children are fun to talk with, especially when they answer questions. Their explanations for what words mean or what they saw happen can be hilarious, particularly when they say a word that sounds like the word they have heard, but it is totally different, and most often has a totally different meaning.

As adults we need to help children learn the meaning of words and how to pronounce them. But sometimes, we don't need to be so quick to correct them. Although they may not be using the right words—or the words we think they should use—

the words they use sometimes carry deep theological meanings and lessons. Let me give you two examples.

My mother loved Jesus, she never met a stranger, and she talked to everyone with whom she came in contact about Jesus. She loved children and would engage them in conversation whenever possible.

On one Saturday morning before Easter, Mom and I were at the grocery store checkout counter. Mom struck up a conversation with an adorable little four-year-old girl who was sitting in the child's seat of the shopping cart immediately in front of us. The little girl was telling Mom all about her "bootiful" Easter dress and purse that she was going to wear to church for Easter. She told about what Mommy was going to cook for lunch and that Grand-Mommy was coming to church and lunch. During this short exchange, the little girl's mommy was busy placing all of her groceries onto the conveyor belt.

My mom asked the little girl, "Do you know why we celebrate Easter?"

This caught the attention of the little girl's

mommy, who was listening to hear what her daughter would say. The little girl immediately answered, "It's the day Jesus beat up the devil. That's why the devil don't scare me."

Her mommy had a surprised look on her face, and this time, Mom was the one caught off guard, and she said, "What?"

The little girl said, "Listen." And she sang, "Hah-lee-lu-lu, He's my Saaaa-ver."

You know what? This little girl was exactly right, wasn't she? On Easter we celebrate the resurrection of Jesus Christ, who defeated the devil when He arose from death and the grave. That, my friends, is reason to sing "Hallelujah! What a Savior!" – Philip P. Bliss, "Man of Sorrows." Christ is our "Saaaa-ver"—Savior—since by His grace we are saved from life unto death.

Christ's death, burial, and resurrection also give us the power and strength to walk through our day-to-day lives and the trials that enter them with the confidence that God is in control of everything; we have nothing to fear. Many of those who watched Jesus die on the cross, thought His life and ministry had ended. However, in God's providence, the death of Jesus on the cross was not an end, it was part of the continuing account of God redeeming His people. That brings me to my second example.

My friend Sandy Wisdom-Martin, Executive Director of Woman's Missionary Union, SBC, tells the story of buying her daughter a bank at a yard sale. Sandy was showing her how it worked, so she put in a coin and it just disappeared. Her daughter said, "Mom, it's an obstacle illusion."

Sandy started to correct Hannah by saying "optical illusion," but she didn't. She thought about roadblocks that come into our lives and at times totally occupy our thoughts, actions, and time. As we look back on those times, we realize that what we thought was a roadblock wasn't one. It was an obstacle illusion.

Sandy observed that the crucifixion of Christ was "the greatest obstacle faced by the disciples." Jesus was beaten severely, had to carry His own heavy cross, had a crown of thorns pushed into His skull, had nails hammered into His hands and feet, and was hung on a cross to die. The disciples saw Jesus take His last breath and die. They took His dead body off the cross, prepared it for burial, and placed it in the tomb. It was over. He was dead . . . or was He?

Praise God, it was not over. Three days later Jesus defeated death and rose from the grave.

Both of these stories show us the importance of listening to children and thinking about their cute word mix-ups so that we are able to glean deeper theological truths. But, these are not the most important things to remember. The point of both these stories is a simple biblical truth rich with deep theological meaning. "Christ the Lord is risen today. Hallelujah!"

The same power that created and sustains the earth and raised Jesus from the dead is the same power through which Christ-followers are redeemed, sustained in this life, and given victory over death as we live eternally in the presence of our God.

Prayer: Gracious Father, teach us to listen for the truths about You that we hear others speak. Help us to recognize those truths and by Your Holy Spirit's prompting, apply them to our lives. Thank You for the gift of salvation through Your Son, in whose name we pray, Amen.

Thought for the Day: "When he comes, our glorious King, all his ransomed home to bring, then anew this song we'll sing: Hallelujah, what a Savior!" - "Man of Sorrows"

Day 4: A Lion and a Lamb

by Harriet
Read Revelation 5:4-10

*"The Lion that is from the tribe of Judah,
the Root of David,
has overcome so as to open the book
and its seven seals.
And I saw . . . a Lamb . . ."*
Revelation 5:5-6a (NASB)

The Lion of Judah and a Lamb that was slain. A lion and a lamb.

In our Scripture passage today, Jesus is referred to as both a lion and a lamb. To better understand this, it's helpful to look at other places in Scripture. In the book of John, Jesus is called a lamb in John 1:29. John the Baptist sees Jesus coming toward him and says, "Look, the Lamb of God, who takes away the sin of the world" (John 1:29 NIV).

This lamb image is the one we focus on the most at Easter time because of Jesus' death on the cross. Prior to the time of Jesus, the Jews practiced animal sacrifice for the forgiveness of their sins. We know this from Leviticus 4:35, as well as other passages in both the Old and New Testaments. According to 1 John 2:1-2, our sins are atoned for through Jesus' death, similar to how sacrificed lambs atoned for sins before Jesus.

In today's key verse, Jesus is also referred to as a lion. He is called the Lion of Judah, as He was from the tribe of Judah. Although I see Jesus as the lamb on Good Friday when He was crucified, on Easter Sunday when we celebrate the resurrection, I see the lion side of Jesus. Through His resurrection, I picture Jesus bursting forth from the grave like a lion coming out into the open. Death could not hold Him. He came forth victorious in strength and might.

Jesus is solid, strong, regal, and mighty like a lion. He is majestic and powerful. And yet Jesus is also gentle, tender, and willing to be sacrificed, like a lamb.

Have you ever thought about that? This passage in Revelation shows it so clearly. The One worthy to open the book was the lion from the tribe of Judah. He was powerful, and from the regal line of King David, since Judah was also from the line of David. And yet Jesus was also a lamb, standing as if slain, according to this passage. He was a precious, tender, innocent lamb, slain for our sins.

What do you need in your life right now? Do you need a lion or a lamb? Maybe you need a strong lion-like force in your life—one that can change your situation, acting with authority and power. One that can overcome difficulties and knock down obstacles in your life.

Or perhaps you need a lamb. Are you in a situation where you need the tender, gentle, loving touch of a lamb? Do you need to see the joy of a happy lamb frolicking in your life? Do you need to remember that this Lamb of God willingly laid down His life for you? Whatever your need, Jesus can fill it. He is both the Lion of Judah and the Lamb of God who was slain for the sins of the world.

Prayer: Heavenly Father, thank You for the gift of Your Son. Thank You that He is both a mighty lion and a gentle lamb. Through His death we can be saved and through his victorious resurrection, we can also learn to live victoriously. In Jesus' name, Amen

Thought for the Day: What do you need today in your life, a lion or a lamb? Jesus is standing ready to help you.

Day 5: Love's Redeeming Work is Done

by Shirley
Read Matthew 28:5-6

He is not here, for he has risen, as he said.
Come, see the place where he lay.
Matthew 28:6

Today's passage is very familiar to most of us. In fact, since we know it so well, we may be tempted to not read and think about it much. But let's take a few minutes to think about what is unfolding here.

Even though God's prophets had been telling that the Messiah would come to live on earth and that He would be crucified, die, and be resurrected, they didn't understand what all of that meant. When Jesus was crucified, those who followed Him thought He was dead forever. The women came to the cave where Jesus' dead body lay, so they could prepare His body with oils and spices for a permanent burial, and they expected to find His body wrapped in burial cloths as it had been left.

I suspect that if we were among the women who came to the grave that morning, we too would have thought someone had stolen His body. Seeing an angel would have certainly frightened me. But the angel said, "Do not be afraid . . . he [Jesus] is not here, for he has risen." The angel told the women to go tell the disciples what they had seen and heard and to tell them they would see Jesus in Galilee.

Our passage tells us the women left quickly "with fear and great joy," running to tell the disciples the good news. I imagine as the women were on their way they may have been asking each other, "Was that really an angel?" "Did I hear the angel correctly—Jesus is not dead?" as they tried to process and make sense of it all.

Now that we have walked through the events, let's look more closely at the bottom line of this event that makes Christianity different from any other religion—God's redeeming work on the cross by which our sins are atoned.

Charles Wesley wrote a wonderful hymn, "Christ the Lord is Risen Today." In the second stanza we sing an awesome truth about Christ's death, burial, and resurrection:

> Love's redeeming work is done, Alleluia!
> Fought the fight, the battle won, Alleluia!
> Death in vain forbids him rise, Alleluia!
> Christ has opened paradise, Alleluia!

Sadly, we sometimes sing these words without giving much thought to what we are singing. When we sing "Love's redeeming work is done," do we understand what it means?

To answer this question let's start by looking at what the Bible says about God's love. "Love" did the "redeeming work." Many times I read articles or books or hear Christian song lyrics about us loving God—a very important part of our lives as Christ-followers. However, we could not love God if He didn't first love us (1 John 4:19).

The first couple of lines of a beautiful hymn by Paul Gerhardt, "Jesus, Thy Boundless Love to Me," tells us about the love of Jesus:

> Jesus, Thy boundless love to me
> no thought can reach, no tongue declare.

The love of Jesus has no limits or bounds. It is so great that our finite minds cannot even begin to understand or quantify it, nor can we come up with adequate words to describe it.

Romans 5:8 tells us, "But God shows his love for us in that while we were still sinners, Christ died for us." John describes the depths of God's love by saying, "For God so loved the world, that he gave his only Son, that whoever believes in him should not perish but have eternal life. For God did not send his Son into the world to condemn the world, but in order that the world might be saved through him" (John 3:16-17).

Now let's look at John's account of Jesus' death on the cross. In John 19:28-30, we read, "After this, Jesus, knowing that all was now finished, said (to fulfill the Scripture), 'I thirst.' A jar full of sour wine stood there, so they put a sponge full of the sour wine on a hyssop branch and held it to his mouth. When Jesus had received the sour wine, he said, 'It is finished,' and he bowed his head and gave up his spirit."

When Jesus said, "It is finished," He meant that He had completed everything that Father God had sent Him to earth to do. A handwritten note in one of my Bibles says, "Mission accomplished."

What was Christ's mission? To redeem us— those held in bondage by sin and to sin. All of us are sinners who cannot make ourselves right with Holy God. Our sin has separated us from God. There is nothing that any of us can do to redeem or buy our freedom from our sin.

But, merciful, loving, gracious God provided our redemption through the blood of Jesus Christ (Ephesians 2:4-9). Only Jesus Christ, who walked this earth as fully God and fully man could redeem us. The "redeeming work" of Jesus Christ does for us what we can never do on our own—reconcile us to God.

So, on the cross, Jesus was saying that the debt of sin each person owed to God the Father was paid for and entirely wiped out for all eternity. 1 Peter 1:18-19 says it this way, "Knowing that you were ransomed [redeemed] from the futile ways inherited from your forefathers, not with perishable things such as silver or gold, but with the precious blood of Christ, like that of a lamb without blemish or spot."

God, through the shed blood of His Son Jesus, redeems the lives of those who trust in Him from eternal damnation and wrath by bringing us into His family and calling us His children.

Prayer: Gracious Father, thank You for loving us so much and for sending Your Son to live upon this earth as fully God and fully man so that He could take the punishment we deserve for our sin and redeem us. Help us learn to rejoice in the completion of Your redeeming work. May it propel us to share the good news with all those with whom we come in contact. In Jesus' name, Amen.

Thought for the Day: "Love's redeeming work is done, Alleluia!"

Chapter 10
Gardening Time

Day 1: The Condition of the Soil

by Shirley
Read Matthew 13:1-9

*Other seeds fell on good soil and produced grain,
some a hundredfold, some sixty, some thirty.*
Matthew 13:8

When I was a teenager, we had a vegetable garden with Essie and Herbert Reece, a couple who were in the church Dad pastored. They owned the land and our two families were to tend to the garden and share the vegetables we grew. Essie and Herbert had a long history of excellent harvests from their vegetable gardens. Mom and Dad had some experience, but not such good and consistent harvests.

I don't remember what all we had to do to get the lot ready to plant the seeds, but I do remember hearing that well-prepared soil produces good, strong plants that yield good vegetables. One day I asked Herbert why he was tilling the soil. He explained that if the soil was too packed down, when the seeds sprouted the roots would have a hard time getting through the hard soil, and water would have a hard time being absorbed into the soil so the plant could soak it up.

In the parable we read today, Jesus tells us that a man is out sowing seed and it lands in four different places: on the path, on rocky ground, among thorns, and on good soil. Later in the chapter, He explains what happens to the seeds that fall in each place:

- Seeds that land on the path are snatched up and do not have time to sprout and produce fruit.
- Seeds that land on rocky ground, grow quickly but have no deep roots, so they soon die.
- Seeds that land among the thorns grow, but the thorns choke the plants and they die.
- Seeds that land on good soil sprout and grow deep roots, allowing them to grow into strong plants that produce good fruit in abundance.

The "seed" represents God's word. I don't know who it was speaking about this parable on the radio one day, but I do remember his descriptions and have added the result of my own studies to describe the four places the seed lands and how to apply those to the condition of our hearts.

"The path" represents our hearts when we don't understand God's word, know how it applies to us, or are confused by the word. At times we are so preoccupied with everything going on around us that God's word has no effect on our hearts. Just like the birds ate the seed in Jesus' story, the distractions of our lives eliminate thoughts of God and our need for a Savior (Matthew 13:19).

The "rocks" represent hearts with no spiritual depth. We can see that scriptural truths help us, but just like the harsh sun dried up the seeds in Jesus' story, when life gets difficult or costly, we compromise and do not obey the word, so we "fall away" from God (Matthew 13:20-21).

The "thorny soil" represents our hearts that want to live for Jesus but may not see our need for His word, or we may just not want it. Our desperate need for God's truth is much stronger than our passion to receive it. Because of all the things going on around us—the thorns—we think there are other, more important things we need to do. These thorns compete for, and often win, our affections and time, so that God's word gets choked out and does not bear the fruit God desires to see (Matthew 13:22).

The "good soil" represents our hearts that recognize our desperate need for God's word. Through reading, studying, memorizing, meditating on, and contemplating God's word, the Holy Spirit allows us to know, understand, and apply that word. Thus, we are convicted of our sin and led to repent and receive God's forgiveness. God's word transforms us into His likeness so that we bear good fruit. The roots of His word enable us to walk through our lives with the strength we need to overcome whatever we face (Matthew 13:23).

When we recognize that our hearts are like the path, rocks, or thorny soil, let us not be discouraged. The merciful, gracious empowerment of God prepares and transforms our hearts through the process of sanctification to become good soil.

We can rest in the knowledge that God's word

will produce good fruit when it is placed in a heart that desires to know Him on a much deeper level. There is nothing we can do to make our hearts "good soil" for the word, but God certainly can.

Two of David's prayers in Psalms invite God to transform our hearts.

- "Create in me a clean heart, O God, and renew a right spirit within me" (Psalm 51:10).
- "Search me, O God, and know my heart! Try me and know my thoughts! And see if there be any grievous way in me, and lead me in the way everlasting" (Psalm 139:23-24).

Then, as we "let the word of Christ dwell in [us] richly" (Colossians 3:16a), our hearts will be transformed into good soil that will bear an enormous crop of fruit for His Kingdom.

Just as good soil is needed for a seed to sprout, grow into a strong plant, and bear good fruit, we must be diligent about being consistent in our personal time in the word: reading, studying, memorizing, meditating on, and contemplating it. This includes listening to biblically sound sermons and teaching, singing and listening to hymns and songs that are grounded in God's word, and fellowship with Christ-followers who encourage and admonish us through His word.

Prayer: Heavenly Father, thank You for sending Your word to us and the Holy Spirit to help us understand and apply that word to our hearts. With the psalmist we ask that You create within us new hearts and renew our hearts to live in God-honoring ways. In Jesus' name, Amen.

Thought for the Day: Is your heart good soil that allows you to look carefully at God's word, abide in that word, and obey that word? (James 1:19-25)

Day 2: How Does your Garden Grow?
by Harriet
Read Hosea 10:1, 12-13

Sow righteousness for yourselves,
reap the fruit of unfailing love . . .
Hosea 10:12a (NIV)

I love to garden. As a child, I toddled behind my father when he gardened. My parents needed to grow our own food when we lived in Nigeria. Our house had an empty lot next to it which my dad turned into a very large garden. Of his four children, I am the only one who seemed drawn to the garden. I loved it so much that he even gave me a small area that I could call mine. He let me choose and plant a handful of seeds and see if I could get them to grow.

I have always loved digging in dirt. I can still remember how that African dirt felt between the toes of my bare feet. We were supposed to wear shoes, but I never did. I especially remember the dirt road in front of my house. If I close my eyes and think about it, even now I can almost get a whiff of the way the dirt smelled after a hard, tropical rain.

The first year I was married, I set out to plant a vegetable garden of my own, though I really did not know much about gardening other than to turn the ground over, plant seeds, water, and hope they would come up. In the nearly forty years of my marriage, there has not been a single year that I didn't have a garden. In those years, I have learned so much about how to garden. I now know which plants grow better in drier soil, which need more water, which need to be started in seed starters a few weeks before planting, and which work best if I buy small plants rather than planting seeds.

When we moved into our current home there was an existing garden area, so of course I used that space for my garden. However, as the years rolled on, the tree that sat right across the fence in my neighbor's yard grew. With each passing year, it shaded my garden more and more. So a couple of years ago, I had my adult son help me put in a new, raised, garden in a different, sunnier spot. Oh, my. The produce from that new garden was unbelievable. I don't know if the success of my new garden was because of the additional sun or the new soil I bought to fill in the raised plot. Whatever the cause, I surely was a happy gardener as I brought container after container of vegetables into my house that summer.

As much as I love gardening, it's no wonder I fell in love with today's passage when I first came across it, especially this verse: "Sow righteousness for yourselves, reap the fruit of unfailing love, and break up your unplowed ground; for it is time to seek the LORD, until he comes and showers his righteousness on you" (Hosea 10:12 NIV). Such wonderful, descriptive words. Sow, reap, break up the ground, showers. God is a gardener, and like my earthly father, He has given you and me a little plot of our own with instructions as to how to garden our little plots.

But what should we sow? What will we reap? We are to sow righteousness, and if we do, God promises He will then shower us with it and give us a harvest of unfailing love. This is the kind of gardening I want to do most.

Prayer: Heavenly Father, You made the earth and all that is in it according to Acts 17:24. Sprouting the plants back to life again in the spring must bring You great joy. Thank You for the lives You have given to each of us and the specific work You have for us to do. Help us to learn to break up the unplowed ground in our lives and to sow righteousness. In Jesus' name, Amen.

Thought for the Day: What ground needs to be turned over in your life so that you can plant seeds of righteousness?

Day 3: Deceitful Weeds

by Shirley
Read Mark 4:1-20

*"But those that were sown
on the good soil are the ones who hear the word
and accept it and bear fruit,
thirtyfold and sixtyfold and a hundredfold."*
Mark 4:20

Early one sunny spring morning, I noticed some beautiful little purple flowers shooting up in the grassy area at the back of our office. Over the next several weeks we received a lot of rain with intermittent sunshine throughout each day. This combination of rain and sunshine provided a perfect environment for these beautiful flowers to flourish and grow very tall.

Soon the purple flowers began falling off, leaving only long green leafy stems. At lunch one day, I asked a coworker if she thought the purple flowers would bloom again. She began laughing hysterically. Those lovely purple flowers I had been admiring for several weeks were actually very healthy weeds.

Those purple flowers reminded me of the weekend my dad and I worked to transplant wildflowers from a side yard to a bed we made surrounding one of the big oak trees in our front yard. We had taken great care to water and fertilize the flowers and pull weeds as they began growing. These plants thrived and grew rapidly, but produced no flowers. After several weeks, Dad asked a landscaper friend to come take a look at the plants and tell us what we needed to do in order for them to flower properly. When he saw the plants, he said, "Brother Ray, you've got the healthiest weeds in the city." Yes, we had spent a copious amount of time taking great pains to transplant and care for a bunch of weeds.

These two stories about weeds remind me of a quote by gospel singer Ethel Waters, "God don't make no junk." What a beautiful expression of Psalm 139:14: "I praise you, for I am fearfully and wonderfully made. Wonderful are your works; my soul knows it very well."

In the hands of the Creator, none of us are junk.

We are fearfully and wonderfully made.

God clothes the flowers—even those pesky weeds—in sumptuous colors, so why should we worry about how we will be clothed, or anything else for that matter? (Matthew 6:28). Throughout Scripture, God tells us to trust Him with everything, for He loves us.

I thought of how sin often deceives us with its fake beauty. We give in to sin's deceitful, yet beautiful, enticement, and choose to feed and care for the temptation until it grows into fully-bloomed sin.

Although we cannot always tell weeds from flowers, by the grace and mercy of God and the indwelling of the Holy Spirit, we can tell the difference between sin and godliness. 2 Peter 1:3-4 explains, "His divine power has granted to us all things that pertain to life and godliness, through the knowledge of him who called us to his own glory and excellence, by which he has granted to us his precious and very great promises, so that through them you may become partakers of the divine nature, having escaped from the corruption that is in the world because of sinful desire."

For those times we choose sin over God, 1 John 1:9 tells us, "If we confess our sins, he is faithful and just to forgive us our sins and to cleanse us from all unrighteousness."

We must put off our old self, "which belongs to [our] former manner of life and is corrupt through deceitful desires" (Ephesians 4:22). This means to put off our sinful thoughts, desires, or behaviors, or "pull out the weeds."

Hebrews 12:1 gives us a little more instruction here, telling us that we are to "lay aside every weight, and sin which clings so closely, and let us run with endurance the race that is set before us . . ."

Then we must put on our new self, "created after the likeness of God in true righteousness and holiness" (Ephesians 4:22-24). This means to put on godly thoughts, desires, or behaviors to replace the sinful ones, or "plant flowers."

Romans 12:2 tells us to "be transformed by the renewing of [our] mind." Ask God to help you quickly identify sinful temptation and give you the strength to turn away and choose godliness.

Prayer: Heavenly Father, help us learn more about You and draw closer to You, so that by Your grace we can discern between weeds and flowers. Thank You that even when we cultivate the weeds in our lives, You lovingly restore our relationship with You when we confess our sin and ask Your forgiveness. In Jesus' name, Amen.

Thought for the Day: God will give us wisdom and discernment to recognize the weeds in our lives and give us the grace and strength we need to pull out those weeds and cultivate flowers.

Day 4: Be an Imitator

by Harriet
Read 1 Corinthians 4:14-17

Therefore I exhort you, be imitators of me.
1 Corinthians 4:16 (NASB)

As mentioned in a previous devotion, I loved to work in the garden with my father when I was a child. He was kind enough to let me toddle along and attempt to help him. I'm sure I must have been more trouble than I was worth, but he patiently allowed me to "help," even coming up with creative ways for me to work. One particular way still brings me fond memories.

We had a large garden where he planted cucumbers in teepee-like structures all along several long rows. The structures were made from sticks or wire placed several feet apart that leaned into each other much like an Indian teepee. String had been strung across these sticks—for the cucumber vines to trail—placed every few feet along the row. It's often helpful to allow plants to trail up onto a fixture so that the fruit doesn't touch the ground. There is a much greater chance for it to get bugs when lying on the ground. This was especially true in Africa, so my father planted the cucumber plants on the outside of either side of this long teepee structure.

Daddy gave me the job of crawling inside the structure with a bag in my hand to pick all the ripe cucumbers that I found on the inside. I can still remember how much fun it was to be inside this amazing botanical structure. It felt like my own secret hiding place. I also remember fearing that I would disappoint my father by picking cucumbers that were not ripe, and his reassurance to me as he said, "Honey, just pick any cucumber you think needs picking. I'm sure they will be fine."

My father also learned to garden by toddling along with his mother in her garden. I barely remember my grandmother because she passed away when I was only six. I do, however, remember the flowers in her South Carolina yard, even though I was so young. To this day, the smell of gardenias makes me think of her, because her yard was filled with them.

My children used to like to "help" me in my garden, and my daughter now grows vegetables and berries at her own home. A few summers ago, when my then four-year-old grandson visited, he too wanted to help me work in the garden. Of course, I let him. Learning to imitate the good habits of others is a good practice.

In today's passage, the apostle Paul tells the Corinthians to be imitators of him, to imitate his ways in Christ. Like the Corinthians, we too should strive to imitate Paul as others are also watching us as we live our lives. Some will choose to imitate us. This truth gives me pause and causes me to want to live in such a way that if others choose to imitate me, the world will be a better place. Perhaps the best way to imitate the apostle's ways is to read his writings and learn from them.

Prayer: Heavenly Father, thank You for Your word whose instruction we can follow and imitate. Thank You also for godly examples of faithful men and women who have gone before us. May we live our lives in a way that is pleasing to You and that others will want to imitate. In Jesus' name, Amen.

Thought for the Day: Others are watching. Be the kind of person others would want to imitate.

Day 5: Gardeners, Parents, and Disciple-makers

by: Shirley
Read 2 Timothy 3:14-17

Children are a heritage from the LORD,
offspring a reward from him.
Psalm 127:3 (NIV)

While there are many things I can do fairly well, gardening is not one of them. I am also not a parent, so you may find it intriguing that I am writing about gardening and parenting. If you aren't a gardener or a parent, keep reading because the same principles apply to every Christ-followers spiritual life.

I was at one of my favorite places to eat breakfast one Saturday morning. I had my laptop open and was working on a blog post. Two ladies came and sat at the table next to me. One was a young pregnant lady and the other a gray haired septuagenarian (I heard her tell her friend that she was 76 her last birthday). They were talking about the young lady's pregnancy and when her baby was due. I heard snippets of their lighthearted conversation.

The young lady explained how she and her husband had started a garden and were growing fruits and vegetables that would make healthy meals for their baby and for them. Then she said triumphantly, "We're ready. We've done everything we need to do to get ready for the baby's arrival and to be parents."

This caught the older woman off guard. She said, "I haven't heard you say anything about how you and your husband have prepared yourselves spiritually to be parents and to ensure the vitality and growth of your spiritual lives."

The young lady seemed stunned by this comment. The older woman continued, "Have you ever thought that a gardener and a parent must prepare a place that is conducive for growth of either plants or children and regularly tend to their garden or child? A parent is like a gardener caring for his garden."

The young lady asked, "How is a parent like a gardener?"

As I packed my laptop and gathered my things, I heard the older woman say, "There's a sense in which you will never be prepared for your child to be born and to raise a child, yet when you and your husband are spiritually prepared, you will have the spiritual strength you need for the long haul. Your primary responsibility is to teach that child about God as you pray he or she will come to know Christ as his or her Savior and Lord.

Sometime later, I was thinking about that conversation and how parenting is disciple-making within a specifically-defined group—the family. Gardeners, parents, and disciple-makers all do similar things. Being a good gardener, a good parent, and a good disciple-maker require commitment, perseverance, patience, and a great deal of hard work. Gardeners provide a place conducive for plants to grow. Parents provide a place conducive for children to grow, and disciple-makers provide a place conducive for disciples to grow.

Out of curiosity, I emailed a friend to ask how she gets her gardens ready in the spring and how she cares for them. Her flower garden is always beautiful and produces some of the most beautiful flowers I have ever seen. She gave me the following short list:

- Get rid of the bad stuff.
- Replenish the soil (mix in organic material, till).
- Repair fences, gates, trellises.
- Clean and repair gardening tools and replace if needed.
- Daily care for the plants by watering, protecting, getting rid of pests, and pruning.

Parents and disciple-makers are called to do similar things as gardeners:

- Get rid of the bad stuff. Ask the Holy Spirit to show them their sin and be quick to repent and receive God's forgiveness. They must continually be aware of the habits, relationships, and things in their lives that are stumbling blocks in their spiritual lives.
- Replenish the soil. Be continually refreshed

and renewed by the transforming power of God, which could involve breaking up routines, changing relationships or activities.

• Care for and repair the foundations as needed. Ensure the vitality and stability of their spiritual lives and involvement. Recommit their priority to individual, family, and corporate Bible study, worship, and fellowship.

• The tools and daily care they need. Ensure they have the spiritual tools they need to live a God-honoring life:

  ▪ a relationship with God unhindered by sin that allows them to be sensitive to the work of the Holy Spirit's convicting, prompting, teaching, and leading,

  ▪ a deep prayer life,

  ▪ personal Bible time: reading, studying, memorizing, meditating on, and contemplating Scripture,

  ▪ access to biblically sound teaching and preaching,

  ▪ Christ-following friends who will walk

alongside them in their spiritual journey for encouragement, advice, and enjoyment.

Gardening, parenting and disciple-making take long-term commitment and work, as well as a willingness to learn how to deal with the changing demands of growing children and disciples.

Prayer: Gracious Father, thank You that You do not leave us all alone to figure out how to prepare for parenting our children. Thank You for giving us Your word, the Holy Spirit, and Christ-following friends to help us maintain a vital walk with You and to face whatever comes our way. Help us learn to trust You more and obey You more consistently as we learn more about You. In Jesus' name, Amen.

Thought for the Day: How are you preparing to be a good parent or disciple-maker?

Chapter 11

Mother's Day

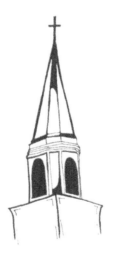

Day 1: Honoring Mothers

by Harriet

Read Proverbs 1:8-9, Deuteronomy 5:16

Her children arise and call her blessed;
her husband also, and he praises her.
Proverbs 31:28 (NIV)

Mothers come in every shape and size. They come as biological mothers, adoptive mothers, and women whom others claim as their mother in some way or form, such as spiritual mothers. I have a sweet friend who grew up in a tough home situation. Her biological mother, whom she loved very much, had six children by three different men to whom she was never married. My friend did not know her father very well, and she lost contact with her siblings, who had moved away. When she got married, she asked me to be one of her bridesmaids, along with a few other friends, because we were like sisters to her. A former high school teacher stood in for her mother, who had passed away from cancer by the time she married. My friend teased that since she didn't have a real family, she made one from people who had loved her through the years, although they were not biologically related to her.

I am the daughter of a wonderful woman who gave birth to me, and the biological mother to four amazing children. My daughter is a single mother to her biological child and my daughter-in-law is an adoptive mother. These two women have given me two grandchildren, one who is biracial and the other Marshallese (from the Marshall Islands, off the coast of Hawaii). These cousins have the same skin color, even though one is biological and the other adopted. And they both have wonderful mothers who love them dearly.

Each spring we celebrate mothers, and I have grown to understand that this honor is not exclusive to a woman who has given birth to a child. Mothers are those who act motherly toward others whom God has placed in her life to mentor, shepherd, love, or help.

In John 19:25-27 we read a scene where even Jesus displayed this understanding that family is not exclusively between people who are related biologically. This is a poignant scene. While hanging on the cross close to death, Jesus speaks to John, telling him to take care of His mother as if she were his own. The words read as follows in the New International Version of the Bible, "Near the cross of Jesus stood his mother, his mother's sister, Mary the wife of Clopas, and Mary Magdalene. When Jesus saw his mother there, and the disciple whom he loved standing nearby, he said to her, 'Woman, here is your son,' and to the disciple, 'Here is your mother.' From that time on, this disciple took her into his home."

In Jesus' day, women did not hold jobs and so were unable to support themselves. They depended on their husbands or sons to provide for their needs. Even as he died, Jesus provided for the earthly needs of his mother by asking his dear friend and disciple John to care for her as if she were his own mother. Another poignant aspect of this scene that is not missed by me is the image of Mary standing at the foot of the cross watching her beloved, perfect child being crucified. To some degree, I can put myself in Mary's shoes. I have experienced times when one or more of my children suffered, and I could do nothing but stand by and agonize. This, too, speaks volumes about the sometimes-difficult roles God calls mothers to play.

As poignant as this scene is, it makes a point about families—they are not always those who share the same genes. So to all mothers of any kind who may be reading this, happy Mother's Day to you. I honor you today for all the time, energy, and effort you invest in others.

Prayer: Gracious God, in Your wisdom, You saw that the world needed mothers, so You created them for the benefit of others. We thank You today for all the mothers in our lives who have helped nurture us in some way. May they be honored today. In Jesus' name, Amen.

Thought for the Day: Mothers come in all shapes and sizes.

Day 2: What Mom Taught Us

by Shirley
Read Deuteronomy 13:1-4

Follow my example,
as I follow the example of Christ.
1 Corinthians 11:1 (NIV)

I miss my mom quite often, especially on holidays. Since her death, Mother's Day is filled with memories of her silly antics and the innumerable things she taught me about how to live a life that pleases God.

Before my sister Anne, her husband David, and I left the hospital room following Mom's death, I stepped back to her earthly shell and said, "I love you, Mom. Now we are going to go and live like you taught us." Mom would probably say something like, "Do what I did as I followed God," because although she always strived to live a life that honored God, she knew she often failed.

Thankfully, my mom was a Christ-follower and understood the importance of teaching her children about God. Mom taught us a good biblical foundation for our lives as she taught us that a relationship with Jesus Christ was our only real hope in this life and the next one. This foundation included understanding God's holiness, our sin, and our need for God's forgiveness. She pointed us to the Holy Spirit-inspired Bible that would help us know how to live our lives as faithful servants of God.

Mom taught us to love God first, others second. She explained that when you love God first, which is shown by being obedient to His commands (John 15:10), then it is much easier to love other people. She demonstrated how to live out the gospel, how to say "I love you" with words and deeds. Mom wanted everyone with whom she came in contact to know "her Savior." Imagine the interesting looks she received as she asked a total stranger, "Do you know Jesus?"

Mom taught us to be strong in the Lord. Because of her deep, abiding faith in her Savior and Lord Jesus, she was a pillar of strength in the midst of turmoil. Because she knew God well, she trusted Him in every situation.

Mom taught us to be joyful. When I teach, she is always my example of a person who exhibited the joy of the Lord. Regardless of circumstances surrounding Mom, the joy of the Lord radiated brilliantly from her face. Those who knew her can picture in their mind's eye her beautiful, sparkling smile.

Mom taught us to pray—not formulas or rote words, but how to live our entire lives in prayer. Mom's prayers were often short phrases of praise and adoration to the Lord, sometimes "bellowed out" in song—even secular ones that precisely expressed praise to her Lord. Late at night I would often stand in the hallway just outside her room and listen as she prayed for each of her family (and basically anyone she ever met) by name.

Mom taught us to be generous. Whenever someone would come to the house or she would go to visit someone, she had a little something to give them. The little gifts were never anything extravagant; they were usually some cheap, useless thing lacking any real value. Yet when she saw it, she had thought of someone particular and it represented her love for that person. Everyone received them as treasured, priceless gifts.

Mom taught us to laugh. She loved telling jokes and funny stories—many were real-life stories that you couldn't believe had happened. She would raise an eyebrow and get that mischievous grin on her face and you knew a good story was coming. That grin was contagious, as was her laugh. And her "tickle box" often got turned over at the most inappropriate times. When Mom smiled and laughed, so did everyone around her.

Mom taught us to dance. If you knew her, in your mind you could hear and see her singing, dancing, and kicking up her heels. She was barely five feet tall, and could kick up those heels way above her head—even when she was in her eighties! She always had a song or a dance to teach you, and it didn't matter if you were the only two in her home or in the aisle of the grocery store, she sang and danced.

Mom taught us to be thankful. Regardless of how little she had, she was always thankful for the Lord's provision. She always said thank you for every little thing I or anyone else did for her. The police stopped her one time for running a red light.

The officer was speechless when she thanked him for stopping her and keeping the streets safe.

For those whose mom may not have been a Christ-follower, seek out a mature Christ-following woman in your church to disciple you and teach you to follow God. My admonition to you is found in today's reading of Colossians 2:6-7, ". . . as you received Christ Jesus the Lord, so walk in him, rooted and built up in him and established in the faith, just as you were taught, abounding in thanksgiving."

Prayer: Heavenly Father, thank You for Christ-following mothers who teach and show their children how to love, honor, and serve You. Help those whose mothers were not Christ-followers to find biblically sound churches where they can be involved and taught how to live a life that pleases You. In Jesus' name, Amen.

Thought for the Day: Women, think about the younger women in your church whom you can disciple, or help to find another woman to disciple them.

Day 3: Words of Encouragement

by Harriet
Read 1 Thessalonians 5:9-11

Therefore, strengthen the hands that are weak,
and knees that are feeble.
Hebrew 12:12 (NASB)

"My wife and I ate with the Judsons last night. You know what Mrs. Judson told me during dinner? She said if she'd had a son, she would have wanted him to be just like me." My friend said these words to me a few years ago. He beamed as he told me what Mrs. Judson had said to him. I could tell it meant the world to him to hear these words. The friend who made this comment, whom I will call Perry, though that is not his real name, was a grown man in his mid-fifties when he said these words to me. I knew his story. I had known him ever since we were young children. I knew Perry's childhood family situation, so I understood why these words from Mrs. Judson meant so much to him.

Perry grew up with a very critical mother. She

had two daughters whom she doted on, but then came Perry, her only son. He was a too-active, rough-and-tumble little boy who never seemed to be able to please her. She corrected him often, spoke harshly to him all of his life, and often belittled him with her words. As an adult Perry told me that he had never felt loved by his mother. In fact, he said he had always felt like he was a huge disappointment to her by being a son, when she seemed to prefer daughters. Consequently, he distanced himself from her as an adult.

I knew his mother, too, and I knew that many people spoke well of her, but sadly, Perry was not one of them.

Mrs. Judson, on the other hand, was an elderly woman in Perry's church. She was about the age of Perry's mother, and also had daughters but had never been blessed with a son. Perry had helped Mrs. Judson by fixing some things around her house, so she had invited him and his wife for dinner as a gesture of thanks. Mrs. Judson will probably never know how powerfully her encouraging words impacted Perry. They were salve on childhood wounds that he still carried, even as a middle-aged man.

Deep in his heart, Perry had always wanted to be the kind of person his mother could be proud of. He had told me as much. He longed to hear positive, loving words from her, but if she had ever spoken these, he did not remember it. Her critical, verbally abusive words rang more loudly in his ears and heart.

Mothers can be great encouragers. But sometimes they can be too critical as well. Today's Scripture passage reminds us to be encouragers instead of criticizers. Verse 11 tells us to encourage one another and build each other up. What a privilege it is to be an encourager. It is never too late to lift someone up. My friend's situation and his comments about what Mrs. Judson had said to him drove that point home to me. Words we speak are so important. They can cause hurt or they can help heal. I pray I remember to speak words of healing and encouragement to others I encounter.

Prayer: Heavenly Father, guard the words of our mouths. Make us consciously aware of how the things we say affect others. Teach us to be encouragers, to our own family members first but also to others You bring into our lives. In Jesus' name, Amen.

Thought for the Day: Speak kind words to others, whether you are a mother or just a friend.

Day 4: Spiritual Mothering

by Shirley
Read Titus 2:1-5

Older women likewise are to be reverent in behavior . . .
They are to teach what is good,
and so train the young women . . .
Titus 2:3-4

All Christ-followers are called to be obedient to The Great Commission found in Matthew 28:18-20, "And Jesus came and said to them, 'All authority in heaven and on earth has been given to me. Go therefore and make disciples of all nations, baptizing them in the name of the Father and of the Son and of the Holy Spirit, teaching them to observe all that I have commanded you. And behold, I am with you always, to the end of the age.'"

I have come to understand these verses to mean that in His position of authority, Jesus commands all Christ-followers to make disciple-makers, through the power of the Holy Spirit which enables us to follow the command. A disciple-maker is a disciple who makes disciples who make disciples, and so on. We are to make disciple-makers as we go about doing what He has called us to do, in the places He has called us to do it.

In the first chapter of Titus, it is apparent that a lack of mature leadership in the church has brought negative results that must now be put in order. So Paul instructs the church on establishing mature leadership—formally and informally.

It is in this context that we find today's passage. Paul is instructing the mature Christ-followers on how to nurture and encourage relationships in the family of God.

From today's focal passage we understand a subset of making disciple-makers is for women to be spiritual mothers to younger women. Are you familiar with the concept of spiritual mothering? My friend Martha Peace defines spiritual mothering as "an older, mature Christian woman who teaches and encourages the younger women."

As Christ-following women, at every point in our spiritual lives, we need to be involved in spiritual mothering relationships in two ways: by serving as a spiritual mother to a younger woman, and by having a more mature woman serve as a spiritual mother for us.

I was blessed to have had a mom who was also a spiritual mother for me, and I have been blessed throughout my life to have countless Christ-following women who have been spiritual mothers to me at various times. These women have modeled for me how to look through the lens of Scripture to determine what the Bible says about how we are to live our lives and view people, relationships, issues, circumstances, and events.

In times of brightness and happiness, as well as in darkness and sadness (Galatians 6:2), these women have lived their lives showing me how to live out and apply the Word of God as they walked in faith through the trials of life. The Holy Spirit used these women as they willingly gave their time to listen to my concerns, to discuss theology, to encourage me to use the gifts the Lord gave me, and they always pointed me to Christ.

It is likely that some who are reading this devotional did not have a mom or other mature Christ-following women in their lives to serve as spiritual mothers. Disciple-making, or spiritual mothering more specifically, works well when it takes place in the context of the local church. It is when women understand God's instructions about disciple-making and spiritual mothering that these relationships can develop and thrive.

The more mature women will be actively involved in spiritual mothering the younger, less mature women. The mature women will also be in relationships with other mature women who are spiritual mothers to them. The younger women will be actively seeking more mature women who can serve as spiritual mothers. The younger women, as they are discipled and learn more about what it means to follow Christ, can serve as spiritual mothers to those younger than themselves.

If you are not involved in a spiritual mothering relationship, begin now to spiritually mother the girls, teenagers, young women, women, and golden-aged women the Lord brings into your life. And please, make every effort to seek out women who will serve as spiritual mothers for you.

Prayer: Heavenly Father, give me a passion to

come alongside other Christ-followers as a spiritual mother. Help me identify women who need a spiritual mother. I also pray you would bring into my life Christ-following women who can serve as spiritual mothers to me. In Jesus' name, Amen.

Thought for the Day: Jesus set the example of making disciple-makers through His relationship with His disciples.

Day 5: The Precious and the Worthless
by Harriet
Read Jeremiah 15:16, 19

. . . And if you extract the precious from the worthless,
you will become My spokesman . . .
Jeremiah 15:19 (NASB)

Sometimes a valuable gem such as a ruby or diamond is referred to as a precious stone. These gems are considered precious because their market value is quite high when compared to ordinary stones. In fact, ordinary stones often have no market value at all. Ordinary stones are sometimes nothing more than an inconvenience and annoyance, getting under our feet and causing us to stumble. We cannot pick them up and sell them to generate some additional income for ourselves.

Precious stones are different. If found, they can increase our wealth or generate income if we choose to sell them. For this reason, companies make it their business to find or mine these stones.

When a ruby or diamond is first found, it is

almost always mixed with ordinary stones and dirt, requiring an extraction process to separate the valuable precious stone from the worthless, ordinary stones that cling to it. The extraction process is delicate. The dirt and rock around the precious stone must be removed, often through crushing, without harming the gem. To be successful, the extraction process must separate the precious from the worthless. This is the picture God paints in Jeremiah 15:19 when He told the prophet Jeremiah to do just that.

This verse first came to my attention when I was the mother of teenage children. It was a time of confusion for them as well as for my husband and me. As they tried their wings and began to exercise their autonomy with their still-developing brains, their choices were not always the best. Our first three children were very close in age, so they all hit these trying teenage years around the same time.

One day as I shared some of our struggles with a friend, she responded, "You need to learn to separate the precious from the worthless." Then she went on to explain that her advice had its base in Scripture and identified this verse in Jeremiah.

I loved the verse and immediately looked it up in my Bible, but what I found did not read exactly the same. I then went to the internet to find the verse in multiple translations. The translation she quoted that I liked so well was the New American Standard version. This is the version I chose to quote here because it pierced me so deeply as I recognized its truth. God still calls His people to do this today in many ways.

Being a mother is not always an easy task. Nothing tugs at a woman's heart as much as her children. They pull both ways—filling mothers with joy, satisfaction, and happiness, but also with worry, fear, and sometimes grief.

There are a lot of pieces of advice I could offer, now that my four children have all become adults, but perhaps this is the best—learn to separate the precious from the worthless and help your children to learn this and apply it to all aspects of their lives as well.

Prayer: Heavenly Father, open our eyes to recognize the precious in our lives, especially in the people we meet. Teach us how to separate the precious from the worthless, and use us to help others learn this as well. In Jesus' name, Amen.

Thought for the Day: God will grant discernment if you ask Him.

Harriet E. Michael

Shirley Crowder

Chapter 12

Butterflies, Bumblebees,
&
All Things Spring

Day 1: Butterflies and Bumblebees

by Harriet
Read Psalm 81:13-16

*And we know that in all things
God works for the good of those who love him,
who have been called according to his purpose.*
Romans 8:28 (NIV)

Butterflies and bumblebees—what do these words conjure up in your mind? A flower garden in the spring or summer maybe, but what else?

They can actually bring different thoughts and reactions from people. Butterflies are considered beautiful and desirable, whereas bees can be painful and even dangerous to any who might be allergic to them. Most try to avoid bees whenever possible. We are drawn to butterflies but flee from bees. This may all be true, but they have something in common—they both have good aspects and bad aspects and they both prove God's goodness.

Many years ago, when my youngest child was in elementary school, I captured a caterpillar that had been eating away at the leaves of one of my herb plants. Caterpillars are not desirable creatures to me. As someone who loves to garden, I find caterpillars pesky little creatures who destroy the produce I work so hard to grow.

That year, at my son's insistence, I put the little guy in a jar with holes poked in the top, along with some of the herb leaves that he seemed so fond of. For a couple of days, I opened the lid of the jar and sprayed some water via a mist bottle. In just a few days, the caterpillar had spun a cocoon. Then the waiting began. After what seemed like an eternity, I began to think the little guy had died and would never break out of his cocoon. One morning as I headed out the door for work, I noticed the cocoon had turned black. This convinced me that the caterpillar had died, but I was in too big of a hurry to toss it out at that moment. I made a mental note to do so after work that afternoon.

However, I arrived home from work that day to a wonderful surprise. The caterpillar had emerged from his cocoon as a beautiful butterfly, one with black in his wings. The black I had seen in the morning was now mixed with orange and other colors and streaked the walls of the glass jar. Of course, my son and I took the jar outside, loosened the top and watched the beautiful butterfly flutter out and land right on the very herb plant that he had liked as a caterpillar. I no longer wanted to get him off my herb plant. Rather, I looked on with joy as the now graceful creature moved its wings back and forth gently while resting on the leaves.

In today's reading God tells the children of Israel about the good things He would bless them with if they would turn back to Him. Among these good things, the psalmist mentions honey. But where does honey come from? Bees, of course. Bees that can sting and cause pain. Sometimes bees even cause death if the person stung has an allergy to them. Yet, they also produce honey—sweet, pure honey.

From a swarm of bees to delicious honey, from a pesky caterpillar that ate my herbs to a black cocoon that I thought was dead, to a beautiful, graceful butterfly. God works good through all things. These are the lessons we can glean from bumblebees and butterflies. Our lives are filled with good and bad, but through it all, God gave us this promise: He works everything together for the good of those who love Him and are called by Him for His purposes.

Prayer: Heavenly Father, sometimes the circumstances we face appear difficult and even painful. Sometimes our lives are filled with bee stings and hungry caterpillars that devour what we try to grow. Help us to remember that You can turn these into beautiful butterflies and delicious honey. In Jesus' name, Amen.

Thought for the Day: God can bring good from all things.

Day 2: Batter Up

by Harriet
Read Philippians 3:12-14

For while bodily training is of some value,
godliness is of value in every way,
as it holds promise for the present life
and also for the life to come.
1 Timothy 4:8

The bat makes a cracking sound as it comes in contact with a ball, the smell of hotdogs, peanuts, and soft drinks waft our way, and people nearby pull off their light jackets while sitting under the warm spring sun. Springtime means baseball season—at my house, anyway. Two of my sons played baseball from t-ball to little league and all the way through high school. Both were pitchers— one left-handed and the other right. I have spent many a spring afternoon sitting on bleachers, cheering my sons' teams on. Neither of them played sports past high school, though. In fact, of my four children, my only college athlete was my daughter, who played college volleyball. Still, baseball rates high in my family. One son even has a small side business of buying and selling baseball cards online. He still keeps us informed of every game and every college and professional player's performance stats, which impact his business, since they cause those players' cards to go up or down in value.

A player or a team doesn't just happen into great performance stats. High batting averages, high on-base percentages, low errors, and game wins don't come easy. These players and teams have put in hours of work, and in the case of individual players, possibly years of work, before they achieve their great records. Long hours under the hot sun doing the same things over and over again may be tiring and boring for these teams, but that is what brings about winning seasons later.

Spring feels like baseball season to me because of all those years when my sons played, but for the professionals it is actually only a time for training.

Spring training.

That term has the word training in it, a word God spoke about in His word, too, but not in regard to baseball. Physical training is certainly a good thing, as today's key verse points out, especially if you are a player or coach of a sports team. Yet it is not the most important training we should be involved in. Spiritual training through immersing ourselves in the study of God's word is far more important, as it brings blessings in both the life we currently live and through all eternity.

At the end of baseball season, or any sports season, the competition is over, and the results are tallied, showing the winners and losers. As a parent of athletes, I have sat through many awards banquets. I have beamed proudly as one of my sons received the "coach's award," another made the all-tournament team, and as my daughter received numerous volleyball awards for her defensive skills. We Christians have an awards banquet awaiting us someday. Our hope is that on that day, we can say like the apostle Paul says in 2 Timothy 4:7, "I have fought the good fight, I have finished the race, I have kept the faith" (NIV).

Until that day, let us strain forward to what lies ahead and press on toward the goal for the prize of the upward call of God in Christ Jesus, as today's reading in Philippians says. It's spring—time for training. Let's get at it.

Prayer: Heavenly Father, give us hearts that yearn to know You better and to learn more and more about You each day. Train us in Your word and in Your ways that we may be prepared for the work You have for us to do. In Jesus' name, Amen.

Thought for the Day: What training do you need to dive into today?

Day 3: Spring Rain

by Harriet
Read Leviticus 26:4, Acts 14:17

*You heavens above, rain down my righteousness; let the
clouds shower it down.
Let the earth open wide, let salvation spring up, let
righteousness flourish with it . . .*
Isaiah 45:8 (NIV)

There are seasons for rain, according to
Leviticus 26:4. In America, that season is spring.
When I think of spring rains, I picture children
carrying umbrellas, splashing around in puddles
wearing rain coats and rain boots. But I also picture
the river near my current Kentucky home rising and
spilling over its banks. Sometimes we get more rain
than we need. In my childhood home of Nigeria, the
rains had a season too, a season that was actually
called the rainy season.

We had two seasons in Nigeria—the rainy and
the dry. Half of the year it did not rain at all;
everything dried up and the world became barren,

brown, and dusty. Then the other half of the year, it rained every day. This daily rain did not last all day, though. It usually came up suddenly and blew over fairly quickly. How I remember the African rains. They were so refreshing and welcomed, especially the first rain of the season when the brown world began to be washed clean and started getting painted another color—a rich, deep green with each huge raindrop that pelted the ground, knocking up the dust as it hit. After a few weeks of this daily rain, the barren trees and plants began to sprout new growth. This was reminiscent of springtime in America and it even began at about the same time in the calendar.

Rains in the Bible are referred to as a blessing after a drought, a symbol of God's love, a metaphor of how God showers down His righteousness, and even as a symbol of how God washes away sins. The words of today's key verse are so vivid. They speak of righteousness both coming down as rain and springing up and flourishing as new growth. They also speak of the earth opening wide to receive it.

My childhood experiences with the African

rains help me understand this description even better than I otherwise might. I have seen the dry earth "opening wide" to happily receive the long-awaited rains.

There is nothing quite like an African rain after a long dry season. I have memories of playing in the African rain with a young friend of mine. These memories are from the year after Shirley's family moved back to America because of a family member's health. The little friend who became my new best friend was only one year older than me, and he lived across the dirt road, a couple of houses up from where Shirley had lived. I don't know how we first started playing in the rain, but I do remember that we had an understanding of sorts. Whenever the rain started, we knew to put on our swimsuits and meet in the middle of the road. He brought toy boats that we would race down the little rushing streams in the ruts of our dirt road. Our road ran down a hill, and one of us would stand at the top and place the boats in the rushing water that filled the ruts, while the other would wait at the bottom to judge the winner of the two boats. Then we would switch places and race them again and again until the rain stopped and the little rushing streams were no more.

We were not the only ones who enjoyed the fresh, cool rains. The world around us seemed to open wide, to stretch out its arms and drink in the refreshing rain, just as our key verse says.

Prayer: Father in Heaven, shower us with Your righteousness and cause it to sprout and bear fruit in our lives. May our hearts be as happy to receive Your righteousness as the tropical world is to receive rain showers after a long dry season. In Jesus' name, Amen.

Thought for the Day: God wants to rain down His righteousness in our lives. Let's open wide our hearts and welcome Him.

Day 4: Render unto Caesar

by Harriet
Read John 18:33-36

. . . Render therefore unto Caesar the things
which are Caesar's;
and unto God the things that are God's.
Matthew 22:21b (KJV)

"In this world nothing can be said to be certain, except for death and taxes." Our famous forefather, Benjamin Franklin, uttered these words. Among other things, Franklin was a prolific writer. He penned these now famous words in 1789 in a correspondence with Jean-Baptiste Le Roy. The full quote is, "Our new Constitution is now established, and has an appearance that promises permanency; but in this world nothing can be said to be certain, except death and taxes."

Here we are, facing that time again in America—tax time. Every spring, US citizens have a day of reckoning on April 15, where we have to account to the government for the taxes we did or did not pay the year before. It comes with absolute certainty, just like Ben Franklin said it would. Taxes and death—they are unavoidable.

There is surely truth to Franklin's statement. If one studies civilizations throughout the world and even looking far back in history, most of them had some system for taxing their citizens to gain riches for the ruling parties. In our nation, we like to think that our taxes are for more than just the enrichment of those in power. Indeed, we do utilize the taxes for many good things like education, roads, and other infrastructure. Nonetheless, though not becoming super rich, many government employees do get their income straight from our taxes.

Jesus had some interesting things to say about taxes . . . and about governments and kingdoms, especially His kingdom. In Matthew 7:13-14, He lets us know that the road to His kingdom is narrow and the gate small. In Luke 17:21, He says that the kingdom of God is within us. He adds in John 3:3-7 that no one will see the kingdom unless that person is born again, born not just of the flesh, but also of the spirit, a spiritual rebirth.

His is a very different kind of kingdom. In

today's reading passage, Jesus told Pilate that His kingdom was not of this world. His is a spiritual kingdom that we are to seek diligently, according to Matthew 6:33.

Of Franklin's two certainties of life, both have a reckoning. On tax day, we have to account for how we have spent our money and whether we will need to pay or receive a refund from the government.

In death, we will have to account for how we have lived our lives and whether we will be able to enter God's kingdom or be cast away. Of course, the real question will be whether in our lifetime we ever accepted Jesus and the sacrifice He made for us. That alone is what allows us to enter His kingdom.

This perspective on what really counts in life makes some of our earthly pursuits appear trivial. How many of us tend to get all upset or even angry over whatever the current politics of the day may be? This nation, this kingdom will not last, and it is not what matters most. Someday it will pass away. Until then, taxes remain a certainty, and though our earthly governments are flawed, we still must follow Jesus' instructions to "render to Caesar the things that are Caesar's" (Mark 12:17).

Prayer: Heavenly Father, as tax day approaches once again, calm our spirits. Remind us to trust in You and Your provision and help us to keep our focus on spiritual things. May we seek Your kingdom with all our hearts. In Jesus' name, Amen.

Thought for the Day: National citizenship is only temporary. Citizenship in God's kingdom is eternal.

Day 5: Moving on Up

by Harriet
Read Proverbs 4:3-9

The LORD himself goes before you and will be with you;
he will never leave you nor forsake you.
Do not be afraid; Do not be discouraged.
Deuteronomy 31:8 (NIV)

The academic year in America and in many other countries in various parts of the world comes to a close in the late spring. People all over and of all ages are graduating from something this time of year, whether high school, college, graduate, or professional school. These days even kindergarteners, in some places, have graduation ceremonies.

When I was a child, kindergarten was not mandatory, so I didn't even attend it. I guess I'm old for that to have been the case, but it certainly was. My schooling began with first grade. The mission group with which my parents worked did not start incorporating kindergarten in their children's homeschool curriculum until I was six or seven. By the time my younger sister came along, she and her friends did have a kindergarten class to attend.

My youngest child was the only one of my children to have participated in a kindergarten graduation ceremony, and it was adorable. There is nothing quite as cute as a group of five-year-olds walking down an aisle decked out in little graduation caps and gowns.

Whether younger or older, all graduating students have some commonalities—they have accomplished something academically for which they can be proud, and they are now marking the end of a phase in their lives while also facing a new beginning of some kind. This new beginning that lies ahead of them—whether a new level of academics, a job, or a new phase of life—does not hold any promises for success. It has to be faced and attempted with great effort, even though the risk of failure is real.

Facing our new tomorrows can be a little scary. Author Tom Bodett once said, "In school, you're taught a lesson and then given a test. In life, you're given a test that teaches you a lesson." Sometimes that life-lesson comes from failure. Or, as some attribute to Winston Churchill, "Success is going from failure to failure with no loss of enthusiasm."

God also has something to say about facing an uncertain future. He offers some encouragement in our key verse of Deuteronomy 31:8 when He reminds us that He goes before us and will never leave us or forsake us. Philippians 1:6 also speaks of God's faithfulness when it says, "being confident of this, that he who began a good work in you will carry it on to completion until the day of Christ Jesus." There are many other places where the Bible sheds light on how to face our futures and the ways God works in our lives. Sometimes that completed work that God is doing in our lives comes in life-lessons gained through failure. Sometimes this work of God has more to do with shaping our character and growing our faith than with whatever worldly success we may have thought was important.

Prayer: Gracious Heavenly Father, You formed us from our mothers' wombs. You planned our steps and have faithfully led us thus far in our lives. Bless those who are graduating this year, whether they are kindergarteners or doctoral students. Their futures are in Your hands. Thank You for Your faithfulness. In Jesus' name, Amen.

Thought for the Day: Today is the first day of the rest of your life. Trust God with your successes and your failures.

Chapter 13

Spring's End

Day 1: The Day of Small Things

by Harriet
Read Zechariah 4:6-10

"Who dares despise the day of small things?"
Zechariah 4:10a (NIV)

"Mom, I'm bored." This exclamation came from my then twelve-year-old son just two weeks after school had ended for the year. My, how quickly a child can become bored. Frankly, becoming bored with the mundane is something everyone experiences, including adults.

Summer is fast approaching. For school children and those who work in the school system, it means a cessation of their activities, at least for a while. For parents, whether working away or at home, it usually brings with it a slower schedule, as many of their children's activities—such as music classes, art lessons, or sports practices—are stopped. Additionally, this break is traditionally a time for people to take a week or two of vacation.

With this extra time can come periods of boredom.

The prophet Zechariah posed the question, "Who dares to despise the day of small things?" I suppose one answer to this question would have been my twelve-year-old son. But the question is a good one to be pondered by all, especially as long summer days lie ahead of us.

What are the days of small things? They are days when nothing out of the ordinary happens in our lives. We are a people who yearn for excitement, especially in today's fast-paced world. We would do well to learn to appreciate days when nothing of significance occurs—the days of small things. In my life, I have seen some difficult days when those I loved were hurt or died. When I compare these days with ordinary ones, I'll take the ordinary every time.

May we learn to appreciate mornings when we wake up to nothing unusual, when we face the ordinary challenges of home, work, and church life. We go to work, come home, eat dinner with our families, help the children with homework, attend Bible study or choir practice—the usual weekly church activities. Then we crawl into our warm, safe bed for a good night's sleep in the home God has provided for us. On those nights, may we be mindful of the extraordinary God who has allowed us to live another ordinary day.

There is another lesson in this caution to not despise the day of small things. I learned about the context for this verse in a Bible study a few years ago. It occurred at a time when the Hebrews were working to build the temple. Back in Zechariah's time, buildings such as temples took much longer to build. The people worked long, hard days in the hot sun doing everything by hand, from making the bricks to laying the walls and finishing the interior. All of this took much time and there were days when it looked like nothing had been accomplished. The people began to grumble about the fact that it looked like they were working hard to no avail. Zechariah admonished them for complaining—for "despising the day of small things." His point was to keep working with a good attitude, because though it might look like they were not accomplishing anything, their daily, diligent work still had value. Their goal would not be reached, the temple would not be built, without their many,

many days of small things.

Prayer: Father, we thank You for all of the normal and ordinary days in our lives. Teach us to live each of them for You. In Jesus' name, Amen.

Thought of the Day: God gives us ordinary days and not so ordinary ones. May we learn to appreciate them all.

Day 2: Streams of Living Water

by Shirley
Read John 4:7-15

*But whoever drinks of the water that I will give him
will never be thirsty again.*
John 4:14

I love the mountains, particularly in the summer. Once we returned to the States, my family would go to the Smoky Mountains for vacation many summers. As we began our ascent into that area, we would look for mountain laurel and the streams flowing alongside the road. Sometimes, when we knew the stream was flowing downward, it looked as though it was flowing upward. There's probably some scientific term I don't know that describes that phenomenon.

Anytime there was an overlook we would pull over and scan the horizon. We could see beautiful trees, wildflowers, mountain streams, and birds flitting around and playing. Sometimes we would get a glimpse of an owl in a tree, or a snake slithering down a rock, a deer, or even black bears in the distance. We loved any opportunity to get out and climb or walk to a waterfall or stream.

One year we were following the flow of a tiny spring to see where it led. The stream got wider as we walked. All along the sides of the stream various plants and wildflowers grew. At some places, little trees were growing where seeds from the surrounding trees had landed, sprouted, and thrived as they drank up the clean mountain water and soaked up the sunshine. We saw little paw prints of the animals that had come to the stream for water. We rounded a little crook in the stream and found birds taking a bath and having a great time playing in the water.

At one point, Dad told us to stop and listen. We could hear a waterfall up ahead. Soon we reached the waterfall that created a nice little pool underneath it where the water collected before flowing on downstream. We climbed down so we could get a drink of the water, since we had been walking for a while and were hot and tired. The water was very clear and cool and delicious.

We decided we would wade in the water, so we

all took off our shoes and stepped in. It was cold, but very refreshing. Before long I decided to sit down in the wonderfully refreshing stream and get cooled off. Before long, Mom, Dad, and Tim joined me. We sat under the waterfall and let the water rush over our bodies. We swam and played and had a great time.

Soon it was time to leave, so we put our shoes back on and climbed back up to the top of the waterfall and followed the stream back to where it started. Our clothes were mostly dry by the time we got back to the car.

Swimming and playing in that refreshing mountain stream reminds me of the account in the Bible we call "The Woman at the Well." Jesus and His disciples had left Judea and were heading for Galilee. They stopped in Sychar, a Samaritan city. Jesus was sitting beside the well at about three o'clock in the afternoon when a Samaritan woman came to draw water. Jesus asked her for a drink, which surprised the woman since Jews didn't associate with Samaritans. Part of our Scripture reading today is Jesus' reply to her: "Everyone who drinks of this water will be thirsty again, but whoever drinks of the water that I will give him will never be thirsty again. The water that I will give him will become in him a spring of water welling up to eternal life" (John 4:13-14).

Getting drinking water for most of us in the States is not difficult—we turn on the faucet or grab a store-bought bottle. But back in Jesus' day, water had to be drawn from a well and carried home. Jesus was thirsty and needed something to drink and had nothing with which to draw water from the well, yet he offered the woman living water. Living water isn't stagnant but flows in a fountain, stream, or river. They call it living water because it bubbles up from the ground. When Jesus offered the woman living water, He was offering her an overflowing fountain of fresh water that would spring up to everlasting life (John 4:14). When we are weary and tired as a result of our sinful living, we can come to the Living Water and be saved. Once we're saved, that Living Water continues to provide refreshment and renewal to us.

Prayer: Heavenly Father, thank You for the beauty of nature through which we can see biblical truth.

Thank You for the streams of living water that You give us so that our sins can be forgiven. Help us learn to sit down in that living water and be washed clean and find refreshment. In Jesus' name, Amen.

Thought for the Day: Do you need to sit down in the cleansing, refreshing stream of living water?

Day 3: Remembering

by Harriet
Read 1 Samuel 7:10-12

*Then Samuel took a stone and set it up
between Mizpah and Shen.
He named it Ebenezer, saying
"Thus far the LORD has helped us."*
1 Samuel 7:12 (NIV)

Have you ever heard the term, "Ebenezer stone?" Perhaps you have not, but if you've been active in church for long enough, chances are you will hear it at some point. The term comes from this passage in 1 Samuel. The Ebenezer stone was a memorial stone Samuel used to remind the people of how God had helped them to fight and win a particular battle.

Memorial Day is coming up. To many, it is just a time where they get an extra day off work and can enjoy a long late spring weekend. It marks the beginning of the summer in many places, with pools opening up and people celebrating with backyard barbecues, burgers, chips, and soft drinks.

But Memorial Day exists for reasons other than just taking a day off of work and enjoying warm-weather activities. Like the story of the Ebenezer stone, it is a time to remember. Specifically, on this day we remember and give thanks for the men and women who have given their lives in military service for our country. God smiles on the practice of remembering and being thankful to Him for the way events and people have contributed to and even helped shape our lives.

General George S. Patton, of World War II fame, is quoted as saying, "It is foolish and wrong to mourn the men who died. Rather, we should thank God that such men lived." That's what Memorial Day is all about—not just remembering the dead, but celebrating that they lived in the first place, celebrating their lives and their contributions to our collective history.

Every now and then, a Bible verse amuses me a little. Today's key verse is one of them. What I find amusing in this verse is Samuel's wording, specifically his use of the phrase, "thus far." The words Samuel spoke when he set up the memorial stone that he called Ebenezer read to me almost like, "So far, so good." And maybe that's the point. Perhaps remembering what God has done is more than just a onetime duty, an obligation to fulfill. Maybe it's supposed to be a practice we learn to incorporate in our lives so that we often find ourselves remembering, thanking, and saying, "So far so good, Lord. Thank You."

This Memorial Day, as we fire up our grills and sit around our picnic tables fellowshipping with friends and family, let's pause a minute and say thank You to God for the brave men and women who gave their lives for our freedom. They made the ultimate sacrifice so that we could sit at leisure and enjoy our picnics. In addition, let's not fail to also pause and think of the other ways God has helped us and let's thank Him for helping us thus far.

Prayer: Oh Lord, there are so many ways You have helped us in our lives and so many people You have placed in our lives to shape us in the direction You would have us go. Bring them to our minds, and may we not be remiss in saying thank You. In

Jesus' name, Amen.

Thought for the Day: God has helped us in so many ways. Make counting your blessings a part of your daily life. What do you have to be thankful for today?

Day 4: God's Mercy and Grace in Our Past, Present, and Future

by Shirley
Read Ephesians 2:4-10

But God, being rich in mercy,
because of the great love with which he loved us,
even when we were dead in our trespasses,
made us alive together with Christ
—by grace you have been saved.
Ephesians 2:7

It was my honor to spend several hours on Fridays with a friend who had early onset Alzheimer's. I would meet her and her husband when he dropped her off for her hair appointment. Then we would go get coffee or lunch and do a Bible study together.

One Friday, our study was from today's passage in Ephesians. As we read and talked through the passage, I noticed a lady at the table next to us was listening. I asked if she wanted to join our discussion. She continued to listen, and after a little while she began asking questions about

God's mercy and grace in our salvation.

Her understanding of salvation was incomplete. She understood that God saved her in the past and that He will save us for eternity, but she was unclear on how her salvation helped her in her present life.

The balance of my Bible study time with my friend was talking about God's salvation in our past, present, and future.

God's work of salvation in our lives began "before the foundation of the world" when He chose us to "be holy and blameless before him" (Ephesians 1:4). As God drew us to Himself, we recognized His holiness and were convicted of our sin (John 16:8), thus realizing how our sin separated us from Him (Romans 6:23).

We learn that "God shows his love for us in that while we were still sinners, Christ died for us" (Romans 5:8) and that "God, being rich in mercy, because of the great love with which he loved us, even when we were dead in our trespasses, made us alive together with Christ—by grace you have been saved" (Ephesians 2:4-5). We come to Him confessing our sin and in faith we know "if we confess our sins, he is faithful and just to forgive us our sins and to cleanse us from all unrighteousness" (1 John 1:9).

When we are saved, we become a new creation (2 Corinthians 5:17) as children of God (I John 3:1), and we have a new identity as people set apart for God's possession to "proclaim the excellencies of him who called you out of darkness into his marvelous light."

God continues saving us in the present through sanctification, the process through the work of the Holy Spirit that we become more and more like Christ. Paul explains this when he says, "he [God] who began a good work in you will bring it to completion" (Philippians 1:6).

Our salvation is also for the future. Jesus said, "I give them eternal life, and they will never perish, and no one will snatch them out of my hand. My Father, who has given them to me, is greater than all, and no one is able to snatch them out of the Father's hand" (John 10:28-29). In our eternal life, we can look forward not only to being freed from sin, but praise God we will also be free from the presence of sin (Revelation 21:27).

Prayer: Heavenly Father, thank You for Your mercy and grace that brought us salvation in our past, present, and future. For forgiveness of our sin, the power to overcome our sin, and for the promise of eternal life through which we will be free from the presence of sin. In Jesus' name, Amen.

Thought for the Day: "And this is the promise that he made to us—eternal life" (1 John 2:25).

Day 5: Bearing Fruit

by Harriet
Read John 15: 5-8

I am the vine; you are the branches.
If you remain in me and I in you,
you will bear much fruit.
John 15:5 (NIV)

My oldest son lives in a condominium that has a small fenced-in backyard with sliding glass doors giving access from his kitchen. This area has a concrete patio and past that is a tiny yard, only about five feet long and ten feet wide. When he first moved in, there was a rose bush growing in the far-left corner that had grown to overtake nearly half of his little yard.

I love gardening, as I have mentioned more than once in this book already. My son is single and works full time, so he asked if I would come over on his day off and help him dig up the overgrown bush and plant something in its place. I love roses and would have chosen to, at least, attempt to cut the existing bush back, though as old and large as it was this might not have been feasible. But he wanted a grapevine that he hoped would trail up his tall fence area and spread out on its top. Of course, I agreed to help him.

The grape vine was so small when we first planted it. The first year it just grew in size but bore no fruit. The second year it sprouted a handful of small grape clusters but then a late frost came and burned them. We held out hope as spring turned into summer that these little clusters would grow anyway, and they did for a while, but finally they turned brown and shriveled up. My son and I have high hopes for the next year, which is upcoming as I write this.

Grapes, like so many other plants, sprout or bud in the spring but do not bear fruit until summer. As spring comes to an end and summer approaches, I am always filled with excited anticipation for the upcoming growing season.

Christians are so like the little vine my son and I planted a few years ago. New believers start out small in their spiritual understanding. At first, they may just need to grow some in their faith through

Bible study, prayer, and fellowship with other believers. But eventually, these same fledgling believers will start to bear fruit. This fruit will build as they continue to grow in Christ and allow the Holy Spirit to take more and more control. Just like the little grapes on my son's vine do not control themselves, so is our fruit. The grapes form and grow if they stay attached to the vine where they can receive nourishment. We too must stay attached to Christ as our focal passage says.

I have been blessed to see this biblical truth play out in the life of one of my friends. Some years ago, an unbelieving friend of mine came to a saving faith in Jesus after my husband shared the gospel with her. I tease that he and I tag-teamed her because she was my friend but when she asked about salvation, he is actually the one who shared Christ with her.

At first, she only attended church where she slowly grew spiritually. After a couple of years, she decided to also join a community Bible study. Before long, she was sharing her faith with her co-workers at the daycare where she worked, leading several to Christ. What joy it was for me to watch

my friend go from someone who had never heard
of Jesus to a person who now leads others to Him.
And the fruit she bore for God is now bearing fruit
of its own.

Prayer: Heavenly Father, You are the vine and we
are the branches, as Your word teaches. Keep us
attached to You. Nourish us and help us to grow
and bear good fruit for Your kingdom. In Jesus'
name, Amen.

Thought for the Day: Grow in your walk with
God and He will bring fruit from your life that will
surprise you.

Hymns

"At Calvary" William R. Newell

"Awake, My Soul, and With the Sun" Tomas Ken

"Before the Throne of God Above" Charitie Lees Bancroft

"Christ Arose" Robert Lowry

"Christ the Lord is Risen Today" Charles Wesley

"Fairest Lord Jesus" Anonymous; translated to English: Joseph Seiss

"For the Beauty of the Earth" Folliott S. Pierpoint

"Great is Thy Faithfulness" Thomas O. Chisholm

"Heal Us, Emmanuel" William Cowper

"I Gave My Life for Thee" Ridley Havergal

"Jesus, Thy Boundless Love to Me" Paul Gerhardt

"Kindly Spring Again is Here" John Newton

"Lovely Source of True Delight" Anne Steele

"Make Me a Channel of Blessing" Harper G. Smith

"Man of Sorrows" P. P. Bliss

"New-Born Again" African American Spiritual

"Scatter Sunshine" Lanta W. Smith

"Showers of Blessing" D. W. Whittle

"Sun of My Soul" John Keble

"Sunshine in My Soul" E. E. Hewitt

"Sowing the Precious Seed" William A. Ogden

"There is a Fountain" William Cowper

"We'll Work till Jesus Comes" Elizabeth K. Mill

Acknowledgments

We are grateful to the Lord for allowing us to collaborate on another devotional. He has been gracious to plant seeds of friendship in our hearts when we were young children, and to deepen those bonds through our relationship with Him and with each other.

We are thankful to Harriet's daughter Kristin Michael, for creating the beautiful illustrations you will find throughout the devotional.

We are grateful for the support, encouragement, and guidance our Nigerian missionary-kid cousin, Baker Hill, provided during the process of writing this devotional.

We appreciate the contribution of Angela Maddox who helped us refine our manuscript.

We are indebted to our friend and publisher, Marji Laine Clubine, for her encouragement and direction as she worked tirelessly helping us to bring this devotional to print and for the beautiful cover design.

About the Authors

Harriet E. Michael

Harriet E. Michael was born in Joinkrama, Nigeria, deep in the African jungle in the Niger River Delta, where her father served as the only missionary doctor at that station. A few years later, the mission moved the family to a larger hospital in Ogbomoso. Co-author Shirley Crowder and her family lived right across the dirt road. The two children became constant playmates. Today they continue to enjoy their lifelong friendship.

Harriet is a multi-published, award-winning writer, and speaker. She has authored or co-authored eight books (seven nonfiction and one novel), with more under contract for future release. She is also a prolific freelance writer, having penned over 200 articles, devotions, and stories. Her work has appeared in publications by Focus on the Family, David C. Cook, Lifeway, Standard Publishing, *Chicken Soup for the Soul*, *The Upper Room*, Judson Press, Bethany House, and more. When not writing, she loves speaking to women's groups and teaching writing workshops on freelance, devotional, and memoir writing.

She and her husband of over 40 years have four children and three grandchildren. When not writing, she enjoys substituting at a Christian school near her home, gardening, cooking, and traveling.

Follow her on:

Facebook: /harrietmichaelauthor

Blog: www.harrietemichael.blogspot.com

Amazon: /author/harrietemichael

Shirley Crowder

Shirley Crowder was born in a mission guest house under the shade of a mango tree in Nigeria, West Africa, where her parents served as missionaries. She and co-author Harriet E. Michael grew up together on the mission field and have been life-long friends. Shirley is passionate about disciple-making, which is manifested in and through a myriad of ministry opportunities: biblical counseling, teaching Bible studies, writing, and music.

She is a biblical counselor and is commissioned by and serves on the national Advisory Team for The Addiction Connection. Several of her articles have appeared in "Paper Pulpit" in the Faith section of *The Gadsden Times*, and in a David C. Cook publication. She also writes articles for Life Bible Study, Woman's Missionary Union, and TheAddictionConnection.org. She has authored, co-authored, or contributed to ten books.

Shirley has spiritual children, grandchildren, and even great-grandchildren serving the Lord in various ministry and secular positions throughout the world.

Follow her on:
    Facebook: /shirleycrowder
    Twitter: @ShirleyJCrowder
    Blog: www.throughthelensofScripture.com
    Amazon: /author/shirleycrowder

Also by the Authors

The Prayer Project
by Harriet and Shirley

Glimpses of God
a summer devotional for women

shirley crowder
harriet e. michael

Glimpses of God
a winter devotional for women

harriet e. michael
shirley crowder

Thank you
for reading our books!

If you enjoyed this devotional,
please consider returning to its
purchase page and leaving a review!

Look for other books
published by

Entrusted Books
an Imprint of
Write Integrity Press

www.WriteIntegrity.com

Made in the USA
Monee, IL
22 March 2021